Change Without Chaos

A Case for the Transformation of Jamaica's Constitutional Framework

Stanley Redwood

Order this book online at www.trafford.com
or email orders@trafford.com

Most Trafford titles are also available at major online book retailers.

Print information available on the last page.

ISBN: 978-1-4907-5643-1 (sc)
ISBN: 978-1-4907-5642-4 (e)

Trafford rev. 03/06/2015

North America & international
toll-free: 1 888 232 4444 (USA & Canada)
fax: 812 355 4082

Written for patriotic Jamaicans everywhere, but particularly for Jamaica's cabinet, senators and members of parliament, the executives of the People's National Party and the Jamaica Labour Party, the public servants, civic groups, trade unions, workers' associations, and for all Jamaican leaders—past, present, and future.

"Human rights are violated not only by terrorism, repression or assassination, but also by unfair economic structures that create huge inequalities."

—Pope Francis

FOREWORD

Set against a background of a crushing debt burden, one of the highest inequality gaps in the world, less than 1 percent average economic growth over the last forty years, and the constant threats, vulnerabilities, and opportunities of a globalized world, this work makes a compelling case for revolutionary transformation of the Jamaican socioeconomic landscape, grounded first and foremost in comprehensive reform of the country's constitution. While Jamaica has been independent for more than fifty-two years, the limitations of its constitution are highlighted as part of its critical shortcomings and part of its failure to adequately harness its human and natural resources sufficiently to attain even reasonable levels of prosperity for its people. The political directorate studiously ignores the obvious, but sections of the population are becoming increasingly desperate as social conditions worsen and they attempt to reconcile their reality with the extravagance of the wealthy minority in their midst, and that brought to them by the now ubiquitous American television programming.

The argument is persuasive: Whereas the founding fathers concentrated their efforts on a political constitution with the end goal of winning the approval of Great Britain, sufficiently to secure self-government for Jamaicans, the country's most pressing problems today are clearly social and economic. The need to address the landlessness and lack of material wealth left in the wake of plantation slavery, for example, and which remains largely unaddressed 175 years after Emancipation, as well as affirmative actions to dismantle the persistent inequalities, have been cited as critical issues of social justice and common sense action to bring the society's historically marginalized communities into the formal economy. In this regard, the work draws a near-straight line between social transformation and economic growth exemplified by China, Canada, Brazil, and South Africa, among others, and echoes the philosophy of former United States President Bill Clinton that discrimination and exclusivity cannot lead to progress. Clinton's progressive ideas are highly respected because of his successes growing the US economy during the 1990s and his post-presidency work in developing countries through his foundation.

Though acrid in its criticism of the inertia on the part of the country's post-independent political leadership, the work is not an attack on any individual or institution. Rather, it is a critical deconstruction of our society, which is grounded in history and the best contemporary thinking in legal studies, economics, and social justice. Its simple, stark, and courageous truths make it an explosive work. It is hard to understand why, given the opportunities and the logic of the arguments presented, more has not been done to move the country forward, as the author suggests, and as those whose names he invokes—like former Prime Minister Michael Manley—did before him.

The staggering nature of the debt, how it was accumulated, the normalized injustices, and the overall fragility of the country, as they are presented here, is an embarrassment to the country and an indictment on our political leadership since independence. This, however, is not the goal. The goal is a call to action—to urge the powers that be to begin an organized transformation or risk a disorganized revolt. This, Redwood argues, is what the country's long-suffering people deserve, and it is the only pathway to a sustainable society. He is correct.

~ **Grace Virtue, Ph.D.,** *educator, journalist, public affairs professional, and social justice advocate; recipient of the Marcus Garvey Centenary Scholarship, a fellow of the Inter-American Press Association, and a Rotary Ambassadorial Scholar.*

PREFACE

This paper has been expanded from an original research presented in the summer of 2012 as part of the requirement for my law degree from the University of Technology, Jamaica. The subject matter was pursued out of a genuine attempt, as a member of the senate, to better understand the impact of Jamaica's legal system on its development. The findings were so distressing that they drove me to initiate a conversation on constitutional reform within the People's National Party, as chairman of the Policy Commission, and within the government, as president of the Senate. The discussion garnered very little traction as the government was preoccupied with the pressing challenges and the immediate concerns of finding solutions to the country's urgent economic problems.

The contents are troubling, and I have agonized about publishing them for the obvious reason that they might create estrangements at some levels. I am now constrained to present this research publicly because I am convinced that these issues must become a part of the national conversation if Jamaica is to find lasting solutions to its abiding social and economic challenges.

Late former Prime Minister Michael Manley said that when it comes to a just society, the growth of an economy can be meaningless if the distribution of the wealth is not equitable. Inequity becomes an even more serious concern when the economy is not growing. This paper raises the taboo issue of the persistent class exploitation as a one of the major factors in Jamaica's economic decline and proposes comprehensive and progressive constitutional reforms as perhaps the primary solution to over forty years of economic stagnation.

Something is fundamentally wrong with Jamaica's society and economy. The problems are so exaggerated and intense that nothing short of a complete overhaul of the social legal system, which reconfigures the interclass economic arrangements, will amount to anything more than another one of the temporary, superficial fixes implemented in the wake of each IMF deal in the 1970s and 1890s and the financial sector meltdown in the 1990s.

There is a major economic implosion in Jamaica each decade since the 1970s and every time it occurs, the people are subjected to unspeakable hardships and the development of the country is set back by many years. Jamaica is decades behind where the society should be. The oppressive cycle must be brought to an end, and Jamaica must finally know enduring peace, progress, and prosperity.

The presentation of this research might lead to protests from some quarters. There might even be individuals who will descend into the realm of the partisan, the petty, and the personal as they try to nitpick or discredit the findings and seek to score political points. These are risks that I have to take in the interest of the future of my homeland. Listen carefully to the "spin doctors" and those who protest this paper the loudest and then ask yourself, "What do they have to lose from constitutional reforms and social justice?" It is in the answers to this question that you are likely to find the very reasons for Jamaica's enduring underdevelopment.

May God bless Jamaica, the land we love. May she prosper and know peace.

CONTENTS

LIST OF DIAGRAMS

CHAPTER ONE

THE CASE FOR REFORMATION

THE NATIONAL STATE OF AFFAIRS

Most societies tend to resist change. Even where fundamental and pernicious socioeconomic challenges persist, many persons often begin with the position that their existing political, legal, social, and economic frameworks are reasonable and practical. In confronting this natural conservatism, former Prime Minister Michael Norman Manley asserted in 1974, that "the Jamaican society is disfigured by inequities that go too deep for tinkering."[1] Although that statement was made forty years ago, Jamaica remains a deeply troubled and precarious society.

SLUGGISH ECONOMIC GROWTH AND A CRUSHING DEBT TO BUDGET RATIO

Dr. Peter Phillips noted in his first contribution as finance minister to the Budget Debate in 2012 that Jamaica has maintained an average national growth of a pedestrian 0.8 percent over the preceding forty years. Notwithstanding this, his most optimistic projection regarding growth for the succeeding two years was a mere 1 percent per annum. According to the CIA World Factbook, the real GDP growth rate for 2012 was actually -0.50 percent. This placed Jamaica at number 189 out the 229 countries ranked.[2] This rate of growth cannot pull the economy out of its persistent stagnation.

The absence of significant growth has resulted in an untenable debt crisis, which was estimated in 2014 to be somewhere between 130 and 150 percent of GDP or over $2 trillion—depending on who measures it. That was nearly four times the total estimate of expenditure in the budget, which was about $539 billion for 2014/15, having been cut dramatically from the $612.4 billion in the 2012/13 budget. $110.9 billion worth of new loans was needed to plug the shortfall in the 2014/15 budget. This was more than one-fifth of the budget. $128 billion in loans will be required to fill the gap in the $641-billion expenditure budget for the fiscal year, 2015/16.[3] Public borrowing is in fact persisting, and at an increasing rate.

For the 2012/13 fiscal year, $339 billion or approximately 58 percent of the national budget was allocated to debt servicing. For the 2014/15 budget, debt servicing grew by 8.7 percent over 2013/14 to $233.4 billion. Non-debt expenditure was $306 billion. By December 2014, the Economic

---

[1.]   Manley, Michael, Politics of Change: 16
[2.]   CIA World Factbook 2014
[3.]   Henry, Balford, Phillips tables $641-b budget, the Jamaica Observer, Friday, February 20, 2015

Programme Oversight Committee (EPOC), which monitors Jamaica's four-year programme with the International Monetary Fund (IMF), was complaining "that the Government has been persistently under spending to achieve the primary surplus target."[4] EPOC said that between April and October, the government had spent $12.5 billion below the budgeted amount.[5]

TABLE 1: ANNUAL GDP GROWTH RATE OF JAMAICA BETWEEN 2000 AND 2014

Year	2000	2001	2002	2003	2004	2005	2006	2007	2008	2009	2010	2011	2012	2013	2014
Rate	0.2	1.1	0.4	1.9	1.9	1.8	2.3	1.2	-0.6	-2.8	-1.1	1.3	-0.5	0.4	1.3

This crippling debt crunch has virtually rendered the Jamaican economy paralyzed and has catapulted the country to economic notoriety as one of the top most highly indebted in the world. *Countryeconomy.com* reported in 2013 that Jamaica is ranked at number 176 out of the 179 in terms of debt to GDP on the list it publishes.[6] On average, every Jamaican now owes over $700,000. The sum effect of this economic picture is that the United Nation's Human Development Report estimated that Jamaica's GDP per capita stood at US $8,300 per annum in 2011 or less than 40 percent of Barbados', which was approximately US $21,800.

FIGURE 1: JAMAICA'S 2014-15 DEBT TO BUDGET RATIO

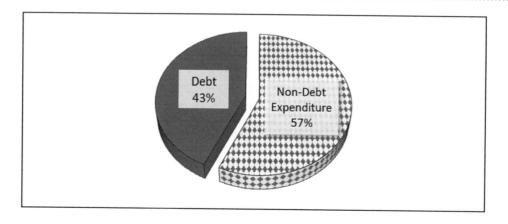

EXTRAORDINARILY HIGH INTEREST RATE AND A DECLINING DOLLAR

One detail that seems to have escaped the economic pundits and the general population is the fact that the public debt stock is ballooning. The debt raced from $960 billion in 2007 to $1.6 trillion in 2012. Despite the herculean efforts to restrain public borrowing, it has continued to climb sharply and surpassed the $2 trillion mark in 2014. At this rate, the debt is likely to overrun $2.5 billion

---

4.   Economic Oversight Committee worried about Gov't's under spending, Gleaner, December 9, 2014

5.   Ibid..

6.   CountryEconomy.com, http://countryeconomy.com/national-debt/jamaica

by 2016 and $3 trillion by 2020. The Jamaican economy cannot survive this rate of indebtedness. Drastic action is urgently required to rein in the runaway public debt.

In 2004, interest payment on the debt amounted to $96.3 billion. Of this, a whopping $73.7 billion was paid to local creditors.[7] This magnitude of wealth transfer from the public purse to private pockets is as unfathomable as it is painful. Why would anyone negotiate interest payments at those unbelievable rates? Why would any entrepreneur invest in productive enterprises when these volumes of returns are available on bonds? And how can a country post any growth under these kinds of agreements? The conclusion of veteran journalist Ian Boyne in his column, entitled the Creditors' Budget, is indisputable: There is an "urgent case for debt relief and concessionary arrangements. Otherwise we are simply rearranging the deck on the economic Titanic."[8] Jamaica is in reality a creditors' country. The decks are heavily stacked in their favour, and their financial concerns are the only ones that seem to really matter in the broader national scheme of things.

In May 2012, the Centre for Economic and Policy Research (CEPR) warned in the *Update on the Jamaican Economy,* that

> [w]hile the Jamaica Debt Exchange (JDX), an initiative launched in 2010 by the government to restructure its domestic debt, reduced interest payments, we find that it has not gone nearly far enough. Interest payments remain higher than anywhere else in the world and the maturity profile has actually worsened in the past year, with over 50 percent of domestic debt coming due within one to five years. Further, the JDX failed to address the fact that over half of Jamaica's public debt stock is denominated in dollars, making it highly sensitive to changes in the nominal exchange rate. This places the health of public finances at odds with Jamaica's long-term economic interests, which suggest a depreciation of the currency is needed.[9]

The point must not be missed: Jamaica has the highest debt interest burden in the world. Even after the JDX, the pauperized and highly indebted Jamaican population was still being milked to economic death to make *interest payments higher than anywhere else in the world.* Supposed it had not been cut, not once but twice? And how is the country going to realize the rate of growth that will enable it to overhaul the rate of interest on the debt? Common sense suggests that since the debt is four times the size of the budget from which it is paid. Then the annual rate of growth must exceed the interest rate for there to be any realistic hope of pulling back the debt. Beyond that, there are only two possible alternatives: prolonged and indescribable hardships on the population or a significant default on the debt.

There is no phrase, not even in the colourful and descriptive Jamaican colloquial tongue, to adequately describe this preposterous financial agreement, which generates interest returns "beyond Bernard Madoff's most larcenous dreams."[10] It is absolutely and completely untenable. For those who wonder why the dollar plummeted to over JA $114 to US $1 by the end of 2014, the answer is the ridiculously high interest debt stock. Every time the value of the dollar depreciates, the debt also

---

7.   Collister, Keith, Low Interest Rates the Key to 2005 Budget, Sunday Gleaner, April 3, 2005
8.   Boyne, Ian, The Creditors' Budget, Sunday Gleaner, May 13, 2012
9.   Johnston, Jake and Montecino, Juan A., Update on the Jamaican Economy, May 2012, Centre for Economic and Policy Research
10.   Claude Clarke, What Will Fuel our Growth? The Sunday Gleaner, August 24, 2014

increases while the bond holders make more money, and the broader mass of Jamaicans is required to cough up even more.

It was clearly in light of this frightening CEPR verdict that the IMF recommended that the government default on local bonds. The only practical way back for the economy now is through a sizeable default on the debt.

On Sunday, February 17, 2013, the Gleaner reported that

> [t]he NDX agreement is seen as more attractive to what would have been an IMF-imposed haircut of 25 per cent on all bonds, said Sagicor Life President and CEO Richard Byles at a Sagicor Breakfast Forum on Friday at Terra Nova Hotel in New Kingston. It would have slashed debt to GDP from 140 to 110 per cent, he added.[11]

This report speaks copious volumes by itself. It is as loaded as a market truck and as clear as a hot Negril day in the heat of summer. No detailed interpretation is required and nothing more needs to be added, except to ask, "More attractive to whom?"

HIGH POVERTY AND UNEMPLOYMENT RATES

Using the base consumption rate of J$124,408 per annum, the Planning Institute of Jamaica, PIOJ, placed Jamaica's poverty rate at 17.6 percent of the population in 2010. Nearly one-fifth of the population was poor by these standards.[12] The IMF, which defines the poor as those who earn less than approximately J$200 per day, measured poverty in Jamaica at a rate of 43 percent of the population or just over one million Jamaicans.[13] That would make Jamaica the second most poverty-stricken country in the Caribbean Region, behind Haiti. The World Bank reported in 2011 that 14.4 percent of the population lives on less than US$2 per day.[14] Dr. Alanzo Smith, a psychotherapist, estimated in March 2014 that 1.1 million Jamaicans were living below the poverty line.[15] He also pointed out that whereas Barbados was ranked at thirty-sixth on the Human Development Index, Jamaica was ranked at eighty-sixth, having slipped seven places from seventy-ninth in 2011.

Statistical Institute of Jamaica indicated that the unemployment rate was 13.8 percent in July 2014.[16] Unemployment has therefore increased since the CIA World Factbook fixed unemployment at 12.9 percent in 2010. Jamaica now has the second-highest unemployment rate in the region.

GROSS INCOME DISPARITY, ECONOMIC INEQUITY, AND SOCIAL INJUSTICE

Notwithstanding the laudable Minimum Wage Act 1974, which legally guarantees a specified minimum wage rate below that citizens cannot be formally employed, and the landmark Employment (Equal Pay for Men and Women) Act 1975, which seeks to enforce gender pay parity,

11. Jackson, Steven, IMF Wanted 25% Haircut on Debt, Says Byles; NDX Seen as Lesser of Two Evils, Sunday Gleaner, February 17, 2013
12. PIOJ Report, November, 2011
13. Ibid..
14. Jamaica Economic Performance Assessment, USAID Report, May 2008
15. Bailey, Tamara, Jamaica's Poverty Rating Worsens, The Gleaner, March 26, 2014
16. Statin Website, http://statinja.gov.jm/default.aspx

the United Nations Statistics Division in 2011 still ranked Jamaica among the worst offenders globally in both general wage disparity and gender pay disparity.[17] This picture becomes more disturbing when one considers that the lower middle class is the most severely taxed sector of the population.

With reference to the 2000 World Development Indicators, the Encyclopedia of Nations reported that

> [t]he wealth is distributed largely along racial lines, reflecting Jamaica's slave-plantation heritage. The descendants of black slaves tend to be among the poorest classes in Jamaica, while white and mixed-race descendants of plantation owners and traders tend to be better off. These extremes are reflected in the nation's distribution of income: in 1996 the wealthiest 20 percent of Jamaicans controlled 43.9 percent of the wealth, while the poorest 20 percent controlled only 7 percent.[18]

FIGURE 2: 1996 ESTIMATED 50 PERCENT INCOME DISTRIBUTION IN JAMAICA

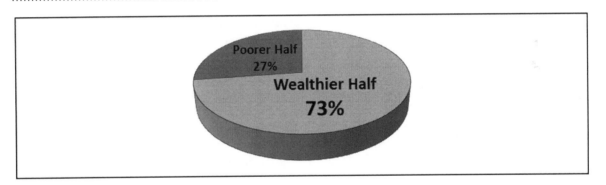

More than fifty years into independence and over 175 years after emancipation, the backra-massa relationship, which existed during slavery, has not changed sufficiently in Jamaica, and far too many persons are subsisting in deep poverty on the economic periphery of society. Whenever these observations are openly articulated, society's privileged classes instinctively assume a defensive posture. It must certainly be accepted, as has often been advanced by the economic elites and their

> No one has to be kept down in order for someone to be kept up.

mouthpieces, that one cannot build up the poor simply by pulling down the rich. Indeed, no one has to be pulled down in order for someone to be built up, but even more critically, no one has to be kept down in order for someone to be kept up. This conclusion is of course related to one's social and economic perspective. Those who have become accustomed to gaining their wealth and privilege from the exploitation of others will have no inclination to voluntarily accept this basic fact.

The irrefutable economic truth, however, is that everyone moves up whenever the base is lifted. On the contrary, in "trickle-down" economics, history has shown time and time again that all that really happens when the ceiling is lifted is that the wealth gap is extended. This invariably gives

---

17. US News and World Report, http://thesocietypages.org/socimages/
18. Jamaica Poverty and Wealth, Information about Poverty and Wealth in Jamaica

rise to increased economic distension and social stress. Some persons are just too self-absorbed and retrogressive to recognize this simple fact.

FIGURE 3: 1996 INCOME DISTRIBUTION IN JAMAICA BY QUINTILES OF THE POPULATION

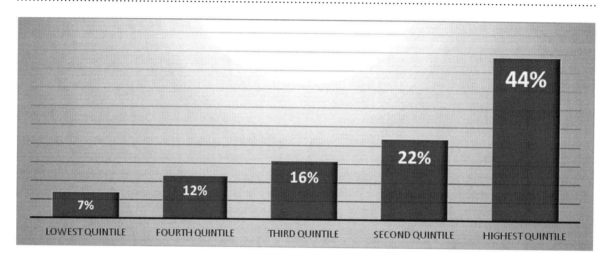

THE RICH IS GETTING RICHER AT THE EXPENSE OF THE POOR

The IMF reported in 2011 that the unequal distribution of income in Jamaica ranked the country the second worst among the twenty-three countries listed in the region. Jamaica scored 59.9 on the Gini coefficient, which measures income disparity. Only Suriname scored higher at 61.6. Haiti ranked better than Jamaica at 59.2. This gap still remains "an affront to social conscience" and is likely to worsen under the current macroeconomic programme and the existing national legal framework.

> This latest wave of class exploitation of the Jamaican people has been facilitated primarily through the unconscionably high-interest debt burden, which has given rise to record profits for the bond holders and low and frozen public sector wages and brutally high taxation on the working class people.

Jamaica's Gini coefficient deteriorated rapidly from 45.5 in 2004 to 59.9 in 2010. This means that if the average income of the poorest 10 percent of the population was $10,000 per month in 2004, the average income of the richest 10 percent was $455,000. In 2010, if the average income of the poorest families remained at $10,000, the average income of the wealthiest 10 percent would have catapulted to $600,000. By this measure, between 2004 and 2011, the wage disparity would have widened by a whopping $145,000 per month to a disgraceful average income gap of $585,000 per month between the rich and the poor. Since the economy has not grown to support this level of increase in the income of the wealthy, this clearly illustrates that there is rapidly increasing economic exploitation of the poorer classes in Jamaica. Essentially, the wealth of rich is literally being sucked out of the poor because no new wealth has been created.

There has been a significant transfer of wealth in recent years. The rich has indeed been getting richer while the poor is getting poorer. This latest wave of class exploitation of the Jamaican people has been facilitated primarily through the unconscionable high-interest debt burden, which has given rise to record profits for the bond holders and low and frozen public sector wages and brutally high taxation on the working class people. These have been compounded by scandalous tax evasions, avoidance and exemptions, corruption, inflated commodity prices, widespread gambling, failed Ponzi schemes, and exorbitant professional fees and charges. Jamaicans pay higher rates for goods and services than many other nationalities on the globe. Record profits, for example, in the sluggish Jamaican economy translates to record exploitation—nothing more, nothing less.

FIGURE 4: 2011 ESTIMATED 50 PERCENT INCOME DISTRIBUTION IN JAMAICA

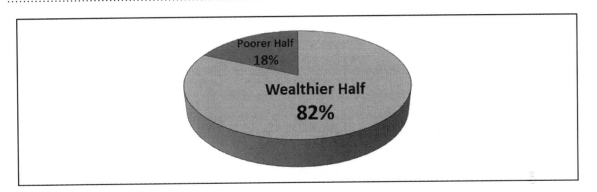

When the 1996 income distribution figures are reconfigured in Jamaica's stagnant economy using the 2011 Gini coefficient of the IMF, the results, as shown in *Figure 4* below, are frighteningly oppressive and unprogressive. Notwithstanding this conspicuously vulgar and increasing gap between the rich and the poor, a new Personal Taxes Study by UHY, an international accountancy network, has found that the "Jamaica[n government still] taxes the rich at one of the lowest rates in the world while taxes on the poor are among the highest".[19] Governments are expected to lead in social and economic justice, yet despite all the chatter about tax reforms, this state-facilitated economic exploitation of the working class has persisted for many years, contributing to hundreds of billions of dollars in wealth transfer.

As shocking as these dated statistics and charts might appear, the income distribution in Jamaica today might be far worse than in 2011 because no corrective measures have been implemented by the government to curtail it and the burden of the debt is being carried mainly by the wage-frozen public servants and the starving poor. The increases in the number of PATH[20] beneficiaries seem to suggest that economic exploitation has indeed worsened. Based on the trajectory of the wealth transfer between 1996 and 2011, the average income gap could race to over $650,000 per month between Jamaica's rich and the poor by 2016. No country can advance with these levels of exploitation, and social stability is never certain.

Most persons measure classism and racism by police abuse of the poor and racial slurs, profiling and shut-outs. The most significant elements in class oppression are exaggerated wealth disparity and constant economic exploitation, which make progress impossible for the nation and relegates

19. Jackson, Steven, Study Finds Uneven Tax Rates Among Rich and Poor in Jamaica, The Jamaica Observer, Friday, December 12, 2014
20. Programme of Advancement through Health and Education, PATH

FIGURE 5: 2011 ESTIMATED INCOME DISTRIBUTION IN JAMAICA BY QUINTILES OF THE POPULATION

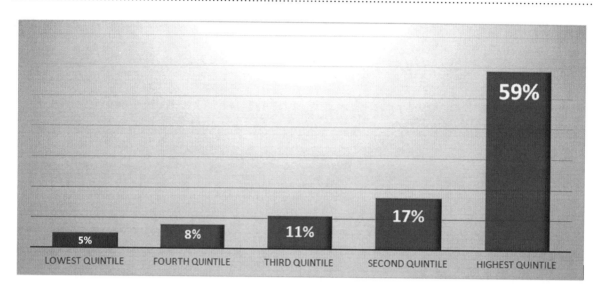

large portions of the population to permanent poverty. In this regard, with possibly the worst income disparity in the western hemisphere, there is nothing subtle about classism in Jamaica. It is unrepentant, unrelenting, and in-your-face.

There is a direct correlation between income disparity and economic advancement and social stability. "Countries that are more unequal tend to be less stable and have lower economic growth." The head of the IMF, Christine LaGarde, also warns that "income disparity can bring more dire consequences too. Disparity . . . brings division, [and] history . . . teaches us that democracy begins to fray at the edges once political battles separate the haves against the have-nots."[21] This is a timely caution for Jamaica. Having recognized the disadvantages of economic injustice, the IMF should also begin to place the same emphases on policies for the remediation of inequitable wealth distribution as it does for fiscal discipline.

PERCEPTION OF WIDESPREAD CORRUPTION

Transparency International defines corruption on its website as "the abuse of entrusted power for private gain." In 2011, Jamaica was ranked at 3.3, out of a possible perfect score of 10, on its Corruption Perception Index, CPI. The CPI measures how business people perceive corruption in respective countries. A total of 121 cases of fraud were reported in 2011.[22] In 2010, the Don Anderson Poll found that "Corruption" was listed as "the most negative thing about Jamaica," easily eclipsing all other public concerns, including crime and violence. More than 53 percent of respondents listed corruption as their primary concern.[23]

21. Eichelberger, Erika, The Head of the IMF Says Inequality Threatens Democracy, Mother Jones, May 28, 2014
22. US State Department Report
23. Parents, Teachers Most Trusted, Says Poll, The Jamaica Observer, Wednesday, September 22, 2010,

A survey, conducted in 2009, entitled "The Political Culture of Democracy in Jamaica," found that "Jamaica is perceived to be the most corrupt country in the western hemisphere, measuring the highest on an index of countries perceived to be most corrupt."[24] Although there was a marginal improvement, to 38 out of 100 on the CPI, the Gleaner reported that Jamaica still slipped from 83 out of 177 countries in 2013 to 85 out of 175 in 2014.[25] Corruption continues to be a significant drain on the national purse and the pockets of taxpaying Jamaicans, who have to pay ridiculously excessive prices for service delivery and infrastructure development.

GROWING GHETTOS, GARRISONS, AND "GULLYSIDES"

The Ministry of Water and Housing has identified 754 squatter settlements in Jamaica. It is estimated by the Ministry that Jamaica has 900,000 squatters, of which 540,000 or 20 percent of the total population, are residential squatters. Former parliamentarian, Victor Cummings once observed that squatter settlements can be found on "hillsides, roadsides, gully banks, inner-city areas, government land, and private land."[26]

It is a very sad indictment on a country that, more than fifty years after independence from colonial rule and over 175 years after emancipation from slavery, one-fifth of its people has remained landless. It is therefore particularly heartening that in her 2012/13 Budget presentation, Prime Minister Portia Simpson Miller signaled the intention of the government to place special focus on the Land Administration and Management Programme, LAMP[27] and low-income housing. One can only hope, in the current economic constraints, that this will materialize and help remedy this historical wrong. Such an incremental approach will, however, take decades to really impact Jamaica's shameful squatter situation. A more radical and comprehensive strategy is needed.

Since there is no record of purchase for colonial land distribution in Jamaica, the government should give serious thought to targeted land grants for squatters in order to counterbalance the economic scales and ease the persisting brutality of slavery and the continuing exploitation off the landless citizens. Some individuals inherited vast acres of the best lands from forefathers who did not pay a single penny for it. These are likely to be the first and most vociferous protesters of any type of land distribution, which is aimed at creating a better society.

Jamaica also cannot reasonably expect Britain to pay reparation for the atrocities of slavery when it has not done nearly enough as an independent nation to correct obvious social imbalances. A properly implemented British repatriation, which targets the direct descendants of slaves, would be more than welcomed, and justice probably demands it. However, a Jamaican repatriation to its own citizens is far more prudent and probable. A homegrown repatriation should commence with land grants to the landless citizens. The price of the land has already been paid in full with the blood, sweat, and tears of their slave ancestors, and it is within the power of the government to correct this injustice.

---

24. Powell, Lawrence A., Lewis, Balford A. and Seligson, Mitchell A., Political Culture of Democracy in Jamaica, 2010, Democratic Consolidation in the Americas in Hard Times, quoted by Gareth Manning in Jamaica scores Big on Corruption, The Gleaner, Sunday, April 26, 2009
25. Jamaica falls on Corruption Perception Index, The Gleaner, December 4, 2014
26. Cummings, Victor, The Problem of Squatting in Jamaica, The Gleaner, Sunday, May 24, 2009
27. LAMP is a government sponsored programme which is designed to provide titling facilities.

It is not Britain that continues to keep so many Jamaicans landless. These citizens have been kept as squatters in their own country for over fifty years by their own politically autonomous governments. Her Majesty the Queen, as Jamaican head of state, can commence reparations on behalf of Great Britain by encouraging the Jamaican government to give crown lands to her homeless subjects. Such an accomplishment would probably contribute far more to the peace, security, and future sustainable development of Jamaica than even a complete write-off of the over $2 trillion of national debt.

A SETTLED CASE FOR REFORMATION

In order to grasp the magnitude of Jamaica's economic predicament, all the indices have to be taken together. Contemplate this: When the entire globe is surveyed, this tiny island state of less than three million people has the fourth highest concentration of debt at over $2 trillion, at the highest interest rate, with one of the highest income disparity at Gini index of over sixty percent, with one of the highest poverty rate, one of the highest corruption perception index, one of the highest rate of unemployment, consistently one of the highest murder rate, and not surprisingly; at a net negative growth rate for the last seven years.

> When the entire globe is surveyed, Jamaica has the fourth highest concentration of debt at over $2 trillion, at the highest interest rate, with one of the highest income disparity at Gini index of over sixty percent, with one of the highest poverty rate, one of the highest corruption perception index, one of the highest rate of unemployment, consistently one of the highest murder rate, and not surprisingly; at a net negative growth rate for the last seven years.

In light of these very unflattering development indices, this paper begins with the redundant presumption that something is fundamentally flawed with Jamaica's socioeconomic configuration. The current macroeconomic picture is possibly worse now than in 1974, and Michael Manley's conclusion then is just as applicable today: Jamaica's conditions require much more than mere tinkering and incremental reconstruction. Jamaica is urgently in need of radical corrective measures to remedy its chronic social and economic state of affairs in order to fend off the growing discontent and the threatening social upheaval. It is law that regulates a society and an economy. The constitution represents the primary legal foundation upon which a society organizes itself. It takes no stretch of the imagination to conclude, therefore, that the constitution is the most logical starting place for a new national framework for governance in the interest of the genuine pursuit of social and economic advancement for *all* Jamaicans and not just the select few.

TABLE 2: SUMMARY OF JAMAICA'S WORRYING DEVELOPMENT INDICES

JAMAICA'S DEVELOPMENT INDICES
Jamaica's public debt surpassed the JA $2 trillion mark in 2014
Jamaica debt to GDP is ranked at number 176 out of 179 countries
Jamaica has the highest bond interest rate in the world
Jamaica's exchange rate was over JA $114 to US $1 at the end of 2014
Jamaica has the second worst income disparity in the Caribbean Region
Jamaica's Income Disparity Index slipped from 45.4 in 2004 to 59.9 in 2010
Jamaica ranks a low 38 out of 100 on Transparency International Corruption Index
Jamaica is perceived to be the most corrupt country in the Americas
Jamaica has about one-fifth of its population living in squatter settlements
Jamaica is the second most poverty-stricken nation in the Caribbean
Jamaica has the second highest unemployment rate in the Caribbean
Jamaica had a net negative growth between 2008 and 2014

CHAPTER TWO

LAW, SOCIETY, AND THE ECONOMY

LAW AND CHANGE

"Law is inseparable from the interests, goals, and understandings that deeply shape or compromise social and economic life."[1] Lester Frank Ward believed that "questions of social improvement, the amelioration of conditions of all people, the removal of whatever privations may remain, and the adoption of means to positive increase of social welfare, in short, the organization of human happiness" falls within the ambit of the legal framework of a country.[2] Nathan Roscoe Pound also advanced the notion that law is a "social institution" that contained the capacity to constrain human beings from antisocial conduct.[3] Simply put, these two eminent social legal scholars were of the distinct opinion that law contains the potential to advance or retard social and economic development.

There are numerous modern examples of the prospects that law holds for the economic transformation of societies. Russian social scientists contend that the smooth transformation of the stagnant socialist legal system into a more robust market-oriented economic arrangement was contingent on effective legislative processes.[4] German sociologists have accepted the principle that the German reunification could only have been made possible through the force of law.[5]

The Canadian (1982), Chinese (1982), and Brazilian (1988) economies also experienced major improvements after fundamental constitutional renewal.[6] The People's Republic of China, which now has the fastest-growing economy globally, has had four major constitutional overhauls since the 1982 reformation as it continues to search for a more effective system to advance its social and economic aspirations. Nearer home, the Cuban (1992) and the Bolivian (2009) Republics attained significant social transformation and economic growth through constitutional reform.[7] The common themes across the constitutional reform efforts of the respective countries were social justice and economic revitalization.

---

[1] Vago, Steven, Law & Society: 3

[2] Ward, Lester, Applied Sociology: 339

[3] Pound, Roscoe, Justice According to the Law, Columbia Law Review: 18

[4] Vago: 5

[5] Ibid.

[6] Constituição da República Federativa do Brasil 1988, Canada Act 1982, The Constitution of the People's Republic of China, 1982

[7] Navarro, Luis Hernandez, Bolivia has transformed itself by ignoring the Washington Consensus

The question must be asked: If larger and more established countries have found that in order to advance and develop they needed fundamental constitutional reforms, then what are Jamaica's reasons for wanting to hold on so tenaciously to a fifty-plus-year-old "hand-me-down" constitution that contained too many compromises from the very outset? Something is manifestly amiss with a legal system that cannot produce justice, contain crime, remedy corruption and exploitation, or produce economic growth. Something is radically wrong with a constitution that cannot advance the progress of nearly half of the population.

> What are Jamaica's reasons for wanting to hold on so tenaciously to a fifty-plus-year-old "hand-me-down" constitution that contained too many compromises from the very outset?

LAWS AND SOCIAL AND ECONOMIC CHANGE

Sociologist Morris Ginsberg contended that law ought to deal with acts that can be precisely defined, such as overt or external behaviour.[8] William Graham Sumner agreed and suggested that law is limited in its ability to regulate values and attitudes.[9] Civil Rights attorney, Prof. Jack Greenberg, has, however, pointed to the fact that desegregation laws in the United States have in fact lessened prejudice.[10] There has been, for example, no question about the effectiveness of the Employment (Equal Pay for Men and Women) Act 1975. Although there is still scope for improvement, it has successfully reduced gender pay discrimination in the Jamaican workplace, particularly in more formal vocational arrangements.

Law does more than codify existing customs, morals, or mores. Law can indeed modify social behaviour and values, and law can induce economic change.[11] The power of law to effect change resides in the fact that law is generally perceived to be legitimate, rational, and authoritative and is backed by the powers of enforcement and sanction.[12]

Social change often impacts the economic structures within a given society and frequently encounters organized resistance from the elite economic and conservative classes. This opposition is often led by individuals or groups that fear a loss of prestige, power, or wealth. Consequently, the late sociology professor Steven Vago has outlined that resistance to proposals for legally instituted changes are likely to take several forms. These include the following:

1. *Social class resistance* from those members of the upper strata who resent infringement upon their hallowed spaces from members of the lower socioeconomic classes.
2. *Ideological resistance* from groups, such as the church and civil groups, which often have morality as a significant point of departure.
3. *Psychological resistance*, which includes ignorance, selective perception, habit-establishment and custom-entrenchment opposition by society's conservatives.

---

8.   Ginsberg, Morris, Justice in Society: 238,
9.   Sumner, William G., Folkways
10. Greenberg, Jack, Race Relations and American Law: 26
11. Evan, William M., Law as an Instrument of Social Change: 286
12. Vago:363

4. *Economic resistance*, which is often the most endemic and relates to fears about how limited resources and opportunities will be distributed and the resulting impact on personal economic fortunes.

5. *Cultural resistance*, with considerations such as
   a. *fatalism* or the belief that only God can effect significant change,
   b. *ethnocentrism* or the belief that certain classes are ordained to be superior,
   c. *superstition* or the uncritical acceptance of unsubstantiated beliefs, and
   d. *incompatibility*, where contentious elements are magnified and deemed irreconcilable.[13] For example, the Caribbean Court of Justice and the question of an executive head of state have been highlighted by political conservatives who want to thwart every reform effort.

In Jamaica, this list includes other considerations such as civic apathy by persons who are indifferent to political processes as well as a pervasive political tribalism which places the pursuit of political power above national development. The main strategy that has been employed to frustrate change in Jamaica has been to distract the mass of people from the fundamental issues at stake. Social change therefore requires political education.

Proponents of radical changes in the legal framework of a society have to be conscious of the forces of resistance. Far-reaching legal change, which slights or ignores the fears of opposing forces, often contributes to social disruption and discord, which can render even the most noble and novel of legal inventions inoperable. The stubborn resistance presented by certain sections of the Jamaican society during the social transformation enterprise of the 1970s provides ample examples of the motives and methodology of opponents to social legal change.

LAW AND THE JAMAICAN SOCIETY AND ECONOMY

Speaking in the 2012 Budget Debate, the Leader of the Opposition Andrew Holness exhibited much passion but a limited understanding of the correlation between law and society, and particularly between the constitution and economic development. He failed to make the connection between constitutional reform and Jamaica's advancement. In his estimation, the proposals for constitutional reform are a mere "distraction" from Jamaica's debilitating economic challenges. The opposition leader should have instead insisted on a focus on those constitutional changes that can advance the economic hopes of the people he represents.

The overhaul of the constitutional framework actually represents the most efficient and effective means of instituting the much-needed transformation of the economy. Law, of which the constitution is the primary basis, is directly related to economic development. To that end, Jamaica will not be able to realize significant economic growth until it achieves a modern constitution that sufficiently addresses its development challenges and aspirations. Without exception, this has been the experience of those countries cited above.

---

13. Ibid.

It therefore defies logic that one could conclude that the Jamaican constitutional framework is adequate to meet the demands of modern society. In the first instance, the framers of the 1962 Constitution recognized that it was a compromise framework. It was deliberately crafted in such a manner as not to offend the parliamentary opposition and other powerful local special interests concerns or British colonial sensibilities. Britain would not, for example, have agreed to a constitution that axed the Queen as head of state.

Secondly, it cannot be reasonable that anyone could come to the conclusion that a fifty-plus-year-old legal document could adequately address all the needs of a complex, contemporary society and economy, and particularly in light of all the serious challenges facing the Jamaican people. The glaring question, which begs a rational response, is, How did Jamaica get to such a precarious social and economic place if in fact its fundamental legal governance framework has been sufficient? If the constitution is adequate, then why is Jamaica stagnant?

Karl Marx maintained that "law is nothing more than a function of the economy."[14] Despite all the other criticisms to which Marxism has been subjected, it remains incontrovertible that law is rooted in economics. Tax laws, for example, continue to be among the most discussed and contentious in most modern societies. It is law that regulates most aspects of the economic life of a nation. Law is therefore integral to the economic advancement of any people, and constitutional reform must address economic challenges.

---

14. Vago: 51

CHAPTER THREE

THE JAMAICAN CONSTITUTION

THE MAKING OF THE 1962 CONSTITUTION

The Jamaican nation was forged in the harsh crucible of the 1930's labour struggles from the ingredients of people power and the spirit of nationalism. The Constitution was drafted by a bi-partisan parliamentary committee chaired by Premier Norman Manley. Being sensitive to the constitution's vulnerability to criticism and the fragmenting factions within Jamaican politics, it is apparent that Manley, who was the consummate statesman, had to suppress his initial goal of crafting a more indigenous constitution. He clearly surrendered his more radical personal ambitions regarding the shape of the constitution in order to ensure its successful passage into reality.[1]

Norman Manley outlined that it was his belief that constitutions should provide government with the scope to achieve the three core governance facilities: (1) the capacity to make law, (2) the capacity to ensure that those laws are carried out, and (3) the capacity to effectively manage the business of the country.[2] The late professor Rex Nettleford also made the assessment that Manley regarded the independence constitution as "nothing more than what constitutions are—working documents containing maxims of prudence and guidelines for the conduct of political life within a given jurisdiction."[3]

It was Manley's belief that "in the end, the constitution is what the people and the Government make of it"[4] and summarized that essentially the business of constitution making was fundamentally

1. a question of where matters are assigned to a person in position as the final repository of power and authority and
2. a question of what checks and balances must be placed on the person who occupies that position.

Obviously, this assessment of who is responsible for what and the systems of accountability on that person are timeless and are still applicable today. A critical third element, which Manley missed, however, was the question of how to treat persons of authority who abuse their positions of

---

[1.] Nettleford, Rex, Manley and the New Jamaica: lxxviii
[2.] Ibid.
[3.] Ibid.
[4.] Ibid.

trust. This remains a major constitutional loophole that has to be closed expeditiously through the establishment of recall and impeachment mechanisms.

Manley rejected the American Constitution as a model for Jamaica and described it as "possibly the hardest constitution in the world that any country ever inflicted upon its subjects."[5] He remarked that the all-powerful president could not spend a penny without the authority of Congress, yet neither the president nor his cabinet members were a part of Congress. He was also quite wary of the idea that the US Supreme Court could void legislation passed by the Congress.

Manley was deeply reticent of the complete separation of powers. Sir Allen Lewis concurs with Manley's evaluation by asserting that the rigid checks and balances in the American Constitution between the three organs of government have succeeded in making government extremely difficult.[6]

In the estimation of Manley, parliamentary government was preferred by the drafting committee because of its popularity across the world and because of the familiarity of the committee members with that particular system of governance.[7] Though he disagreed, Manley was conscious that the perception was generally held that elected representatives who were not ministers did not have much power. He was also very aware that the best minds would not always come into political life and expressed the hope that more people would eventually choose to participate in the public life of the country.[8] However, the practical business of running a country cannot be built upon mere optimism.

PARTIAL SEPARATION OF POWERS

Ironically, Michael Manley, who was Norman Manley's son and successor as leader of the political party he helped establish, did not share his father's perspectives on this issue. Michael Manley expressed the frustration as prime minister that the uncritical transplanting of the Westminster parliamentary model "placed an unnecessary constraint upon the ability of government to draw upon the widest reservoir of committed talent in forming the components of a government of change." He considered it "an idle imposition to limit the search for ministerial talent." It was his view that it also had the added negative element of reducing the time ministers could spend with their constituents. In the increasing complexity of running a government, this has become an even greater handicap and complaint today.

It was Michael Manley's opinion that the wholesale Westminster transplant did not consider that Jamaica had only 10 percent of the more than six hundred members of the British Parliament with similar intricacies in the business of managing public affairs.[9] He concluded that a constitutional amendment, which gave greater freedom in ministerial appointments, would promote greater flexibility and efficiency. Clearly, the multifarious demands of a modern government warrant a review of this 1974 proposal for a constitutional amendment.

---

5.   Ibid.
6.   Lewis, Allen, The Separation of Powers: Its Relevance Parliamentary Democracy (1978) WILJ 4
7.   Nettleford, Rex, Manley and the New Jamaica: 300–301
8.   Ibid.
9.   Manley, Michael, Politics of Change: 188-190

Norman Manley's challenge with the representation of the executive in the legislature can quite easily be resolved through an indigenized republican system with partial separation of powers between the legislature and the executive. This approach can mandate that a predetermined number of cabinet members shall be members of parliament and that certain critical ministerial posts—such as finance, human rights, public service, economic development, and national security—be occupied by sitting representatives in the house of parliament. In any event, these ministers ought to be readily available to provide answers to the people's representatives in parliament. Obviously, this kind of parliamentary configuration would require an executive House Speaker and a less ceremonial Senate President. The leader of government business in both houses could also be cabinet members, even with minority representation in the house of parliament.

Although a minority executive might be required to work harder to build consensus to get support in parliament, the cabinet would still be able to set the legislative agenda to meet national development goals. Evidently, political compromise might well be the will of a population that elects a minority prime minister. Minority representation in parliament does not have to create a lame duck prime minister or become an unwelcomed "millstone around the neck" of the cabinet. A partial separation of powers would also resolve Michael Manley's "idle imposition" critique by granting the prime minister the latitude to broaden the search for ministerial talents. It might even create the possibility for interparty ministerial search.

MISSION UNACCOMPLISHED

National Hero, Rt. Excellent Norman Washington Manley has come to be widely regarded as the "father of the nation" because of his pioneering role and astute leadership in the push for independence under his stewardship as premier of Jamaica during the 1950s. He outlined that the principal concerns of the framers of the 1962 Constitution were decolonization and independence.

In his "Mission Accomplished" farewell address to the People's National Party conference in 1969, Manley, in his often-quoted declaration, explained that the mission of his generation was "to win self-government for Jamaica. To win political power . . ." He further stressed that the mission of the generation that succeeded his was to use that hard-won political power to tackle "the job of reconstructing the social and economic society and life of Jamaica."[10] That latter mission is obviously still pending.

The drafters of the 1962 Constitution had set out to achieve a "political constitution." That was their focus. The major challenges with which Jamaica contends today are social and economic in nature and urgently require a constitution which focuses on those considerations. A "political constitution," such as is currently in force in Jamaica, concentrates its parliament's law-making concerns primarily on "peace, order, and good government."[11] In such a context, "order" could simply mean the preservation of the prevailing systems—whatever they might be, and the avoidance of social disorder.

[10.] Nettleford, Rex, Manley and the New Jamaica: 380–381
[11.] Section 49(1), The Jamaican Constitution

> The primary obligation a government has towards its people is to ensure that social and economic justice is done to, for, and by all its people, and that economic development is attained and sustained.

Armed with such a constitution and the resultant operational laws and Force Orders, the police force, for example, is not required or challenged beyond discretion to give effect to broader justice issues. The basic duties of the Jamaica Constabulary Force, JCF, regardless of other underlying social concerns, are the maintenance of law and order, the protection of life and property, the prevention and detection of crime, and the preservation of peace.[12] Although the JCF proposes in its mission statement to "serve, protect, and reassure with courtesy, integrity, and with proper respect for the rights of all," those noble intentions are limited to what the constitution promulgates and enforces. Under the present constitution, the JCF has no mandate to apply social justice considerations. The efforts of those civil groups that dedicate their time to pursuing constraints on police excesses would be much better served in pursuit of a legal framework, which compels police personnel to recognize themselves as paid public agents of justice for law-abiding people of the state.

A "social and economic constitution" is principally concerned about social justice and economic development. Within such a structure, the primary obligation a government has toward its people is to ensure that social and economic justice is done to, for, and by *all* its people, and that economic development is attained and sustained. Jamaica is critically in need of such a constitution and such a focus from all the branches and agencies of the government. In other words, Jamaica urgently needs a constitution that will concentrate on the remedies for social injustice and economic stagnation.

TENSIONS IN THE JAMAICAN CONSTITUTION

In the mind of Norman Manley, constitutions provided a framework for good governance and the preservation of the rights of the people. However, he also painstakingly emphasized the need for the constitution to set out the purpose and intentions of the government.[13] He concluded that in the end, the constitution must be used "to build a better land for all Jamaica, to create more happiness for its people, and a country which offers opportunities of real life to all men and women and young people, that they may see in their country a future in the world."[14] And hasn't that been one of Jamaica's greatest developmental blemishes, that far too many of its citizens have not, and still cannot, see in their country a future in the world?

> The constitution must be used "to build a better land for all Jamaica, to create more happiness for its people, and a country which offers opportunities of real life to all men and women and young people, that they may see in their country a future in the world." —Norman Manley

The World Bank fixed Jamaica's percentage migration among tertiary graduates for the decade ending 1990 at 85.5 percent and 84.7 percent for the decade ending in the year 2000.[15] This

---

12. The Mission Statement of the Jamaica Constabulary Force
13. Ibid.
14. Ibid.
15. Trading Economics, Net Migration in Jamaica, http://www.tradingeconomics.com/jamaica/net-migration-wb-data.html

is an alarming rate of brain drain and clearly runs counter to Norman Manley's hope that the constitution would have helped to create a Jamaica that would have provided more opportunities for its citizens. If Manley was correct that the constitution can be used as a tool for a prosperous Jamaica, then the constitution should be revisited and reshaped to deliver on this promise of "opportunities of real life to all men and women and young people."

In light of this, the emphases on the removal of the Queen as head of state and the implementation of the Caribbean Court of Justice as Jamaica's final court of appeal, though evidently well-intentioned, are misplaced and might in fact be "distractions" from the core business of crafting a constitution that addresses the pressing practical challenges of the contemporary Jamaican society. What Jamaica needs most is a constitution that advances a framework for the rapid resolution of its myriad of debilitating social and economic challenges.

More than fifty years on, it is apparent that Jamaica has not fully actualized the promise of its independence. The obvious challenges that are presented from this conclusion are, first, to understand the factors that have given rise to the derailment of the independence dream, and second, to propose pragmatic solutions for the resurrection of the hope of the founding fathers of the nation.

PERSONAL INDEPENDENCE VERSUS NATIONAL INDEPENDENCE

Independence is both collective and individual. It should provide scope for both national and personal autonomy and advancement. Genuine development is mutually contingent on both personal and national progress because no nation can accurately lay claim to any development that leaves large masses of its people behind the agenda for development. Independence must indeed offer "real life opportunities" for self-determination and self-actualization "to *all* men, women and young people."

> Jamaica, has not reached the stage for tinkering or retirement thinking. The country is urgently in need of a radical society-changing transformation of a scope which must exceed the combined efforts of the 1950s and 1970s if any tangible progress is to be realized.

Consequently, the life of a nation often mirrors the development of human beings. The birth of a nation at independence is naturally an unsettling time of forging new relationships and finding one's place in the world. Jamaica's turbulent adolescent period during the 1970s pushed the frontiers of independence against the reluctance of the residual "parental" colonial controls at home and abroad. At over fifty years old, the Jamaican political culture is now being dominated by a tinkering, retirement-planning mentality. Jamaica, however, has not reached the stage for tinkering or retirement thinking. The country is urgently in need of a radical, society-changing transformation of a scope that must exceed the combined efforts of the 1950s and 1970s if any tangible progress is to be realized.

In the past, the struggle for real independence was waged against international neocolonial forces. However, there is an even more intense ongoing national struggle against the local colonial elements that are determined to keep the broader mass of people "in their damn places," bereft of the promises of real independence, so that they can be milked of their talents, labour, and resources. During the 1970s, this turbulent struggle by the "common mass of the people" was played out in the search for equality of opportunities in practical terms, such as the quests for better wages and working conditions, improved housing, more access to education, the right to productive lands, and decent social amenities as well as other more transcendent human pursuits such as equal status for children, gender parity, and social equality.

The Michael Manley–led government from 1972 to 1980 championed the first real and only significant thrust for the personal independence of the people of Jamaica. It gave cause to a raft of new legislative provisions such as the Status of Children Act, the Equal Pay Act, the Minimum Wage Act, and programmes and institutions such as free university education, Project Land Lease, and the National Housing Trust. Despite these creditable pursuits, Jamaica's abiding and disturbing development indices indicate clearly that it is on the home front of the struggle for personal freedom that the promise of independence and the dream of a better Jamaica for all its citizens has been fought and lost. The government of the 1970s also clearly dropped the ball on constitutional reforms. The labour laws and land reform laws, for example, should have been embedded in the constitution. Evidently, too, the land lease programme should have been a land ownership programme.

The 1970s brought to the fore the fact that the independence that Jamaica requires most is not liberation from international colonial forces. The broader mass of the Jamaican population is in dire need of freedom from internal economic oppression, constricting social opportunities, public mismanagement, and private and public corruption. Constitutional reform that concentrates on the lesser battle of decolonization or the "completion of Jamaica's independence" is likely to attract the types of cynicism demonstrated by the leader of the opposition in his response to the proposed constitutional tinkering in the 2012 budget debate.

The truth is that the constitution, to its credit, has been able to give birth to a relatively stable and democratic political system. The politics of the constitution, though not ideal, is decent. Therefore even where such perspectives are well meaning, any focus on the political elements of the constitution will indeed appear to be a "distraction" from the resolution of the emerging sense of haplessness, hopelessness, and civic apathy that is becoming self-evident among the greater masses of the population. These are the issues that constitutional reform must address as priority. A new constitution must forcefully engage the leaders and the entire population in legally enforceable systems of patriotic commitment to social and economic justice, productivity, and personal and public accountability.

EQUALITY VERSUS CLASSISM

The naked truth is that because of the concessions and compromises that were made to the powerful local colonial forces, the constitution did not go far enough in addressing the inequitable class and economic arrangements that existed in 1962. The constitution proposed equality but legitimized inequality, for example, by entrenching property rights in a context where too many of the people were landless. This continues to be played out in the proliferation of shantytowns, squatter settlements, "gullysides," and ghettos, which are the breeding grounds for garrisons and the festering points of crime and violence. Essentially, the constitution has required the people to compete with the inequitable rules that have been unwittingly enshrined therein. A society that forces people to live like animals should not feign alarm when they do not behave like human beings.

The rules for life in Jamaica were stacked against the broader mass of the population from the very onset of independence. There can be no resolution of the social conditions until the laws are reframed to level the playing field. Garrisons will not be dismantled by "walk-throughs" by political leaders. They will be undone by constitutionally sanctioned affirmative action laws, which are enforced to provide land, reasonable access to decent housing, humane community standards, and the general socioeconomic advancement for the residents of these communities. The right to a decent life for all citizens cannot be left to the charity of others. The constitution must guarantee the planned development of its most vulnerable communities and citizens through affirmative action. The constitution must also render it a national shame on cabinets that govern over economic injustice and on members of parliament who preside over squalor. Destitution and the factors that give rise to it must be summarily outlawed by the constitution.

Discussions about the persistent problems of class and race have been rendered taboo in the quest for "political correctness." Jamaica has chosen to deal with the abiding classism by ignoring the fact that it exists and the fact that it continues to be a major developmental challenge in the contemporary Jamaican reality. No issue is ever resolved by sweeping it under the carpet; and anyone who cannot understand the class, race and colour dynamics of a country cannot understand the politics, economics, or even the religious perspectives of that society and will not be able to remedy its ills.

> The Charter "has a lot of bark but very little bite."
>
> — Edward Seaga

The Charter of Fundamental Rights and Freedoms, which has replaced the Bill of Rights in the constitution, proposes equality before the law, supposedly to redress the issues of the social distinctions. However, the constitution does not activate the legislative, social, and economic mechanisms by which that equality can be attained. Cabinet and the state agencies are not properly held to account by the Charter of Rights.

At the joint sitting of the houses of parliament in his honour, former Prime Minister Edward Seaga concluded that the much-touted charter "has a lot of bark but very little bite"[16] because the constitution has not instituted enforceable penalties or regulatory systems to constrain and remedy breaches. It offers no affirmative action provisions for marginalized and excluded Jamaicans in order to ensure a leveling of the socioeconomic playing field. To this end, the charter could well be considered a constitutional façade.

The Charter of Rights will continue to have very little relevance for the vast majority of Jamaicans who cannot afford high-powered constitutional lawyers or access the court system. Yet ostensibly, if not paradoxically, it is for the socially and economically defenseless that these laws were enacted. This irony is typical of the "three card" that is entrenched in our constitutional and legal framework. The lofty laws that have been created for the people often benefit them very little, if at all. Those who would question this conclusion should get out of their supercilious hilltop mansions, wind down their extravagant SUV windows, and take a good, hard look at the grossly inequitable social reality, which is "Jamaica, land we love."

[16.] Seaga, Edward, Presentation to Parliament, October 9, 2012

IDEOLOGICAL INDEPENDENCE VERSUS REAL INDEPENDENCE

Ideas generate action, and it is from ideology that programmes evolve. When the people gave up the ideological struggle for personal independence around 1978 and finally surrendered in 1980, Jamaica lost an opportunity for real independence. The struggle has been suspended since, and consequently, the income gap has persisted and is rapidly expanding, making Jamaica one of the most economically unequalled societies in the entire world. Social development has been stymied, economic growth has stagnated, the public debt has ballooned, and social tensions have escalated. When the government has to cut back on capital development in one of the worst periods of social decline, do not expect that anything will change anytime soon. The sad reality is that Jamaica is literally subsisting on a borrowed existence, on borrowed time, with borrowed money. The Jamaican society is in fact a ticking time bomb.

Anthropologist Don Robotham has concurred with this prognosis of the Jamaican socioeconomic landscape. In his column in the *Sunday Gleaner* of October 21, 2012, entitled, *Jamaica on the Brink*, he declared Jamaica an economic disaster zone. He stated that, "Jamaica is on the brink of an unprecedented disaster. We are at the very edge of the precipice. If urgent action is not taken, we will tumble into the ravine with disastrous results."[17]

Although he described the stark economic reality for approximately one million Jamaicans who subsist daily from hand-to-mouth, Professor Robotham, who is at pains to explain that he is not an alarmist, believes that the threatening economic crisis could unfold in the following manner:

> Be clear what this will mean: the public and private sectors will cave; thousands, possibly hundreds of thousands, will be laid off; the education and health systems, both public and private, will shut down. Banks will go bust. Life savings will be wiped out, whether in local or foreign currencies. Pensions gone, everything will crash.

> Supermarket shelves will become bare and gas will disappear from the stations. Prices will soar as the exchange rate zooms off into the stratosphere. Simple things which you currently take for granted—visiting a friend, going to a football game, playing a game of dominoes, going shopping, going to church—will become major challenges as everyone ruthlessly scrambles for survival. Crime rates will go through the roof. Our entire institutional structure and way of life will have had the rug pulled from under it. It will collapse.[18]

There are the select few who benefit the most from the persistent economic injustice, particularly the high-interest debt regime who continue, with the assistance of successive governments, like an insatiable vampire, to suck the lifeblood out of the wider population. The comfortable members of the upper middle class have inoculated and insulated themselves with "record profits" from the suffering of the general population. They are perhaps blinded to these ominous economic signals and ridicule anyone who calls attention to the suffering of the people. Some politicians appear to wear the same economic rose-tinted glasses and continue to paint grand pictures of an imminent and glorious future and wonder what the fuss is all about. No doubt some will even attribute the charge of "laziness" as the reason for the underdevelopment of the people.

---

17. Robotham, Don, Jamaica on the Brink, In Focus, The Sunday Gleaner, October 21, 2012
18. Ibid.

Edward Seaga has warned that although the frills, which are enjoyed by the upper echelons of society, may indicate progress, the fundamentals do not.[19] The frills seem to have blinded the beneficiaries of the crooked economy, because few have attempted to break the back of the unrelenting economic exploitation of the Jamaican people by the privileged few. Our leaders have not been able to chart a stable economic course for the country because development cannot result from oppression. Some have even actively contributed to the persistence of poverty through misguided policies and strategies such as the amassing of the ridiculously high-interest debt burden.

Development and oppression are antonyms—philosophically as well as practically. They cannot coexist in the same national space. This assertion was affirmed most emphatically at the Democratic National Conference on September 5, 2012, when former US President Bill Clinton declared that

> [i]t turns out that advancing equal opportunity and economic empowerment is both morally right and good economics. Why? Because poverty, discrimination and ignorance restrict growth. When you stifle human potential, when you don't invest in new ideas, it doesn't just cut off the people who are affected; it hurts us all.[20]

If Bill Clinton is right, then trickle-down economics is unquestionably very bad economics and even worse politics. Ample evidence of this can be found in Jamaica's political history. Despite posting the two best periods of "economic growth" in the late 1960s and the late 1980s, both administrations were unceremoniously hounded from power in massive defeats because the growth figures did not translate into a better quality of life for the vast majority of the people. The current administration is far too focused on the blind pursuit of a macroeconomic fix. The concomitant and dogmatic structural adjustments and austerity measures, with the "debt-repayment-first growth-later policy"[21] have left very little scope for social or economic investments. Again, this is underscored by the cuts in capital development and reduced government spending.

The macroeconomic-stability-without-development approach is hardly different from the trickle-down, growth-without-development economics because structural adjustments always stifle the human potential of a nation. The half-starving public sector workers will have to defer their aspirations for wages that can match the rate of inflation, but the filthy rich public creditors are likely to be paid in full and on time. The human misery with its debilitating long-term practical and psycho-social consequences inherent in the general postponement of development, and the inevitable cost of social remediation, will have to be borne over many long years into the future. The seven-year struggle with the current, unrelenting economic predicament confirms this.

There is no quick fix for decades of humongous high-interest debt or for structural adjustments. There is no quick economic fix either, and the government should have pursued a more gradual and less painful process. Reduced spending on education and training, the heavy toll from the criminality that is bred, the rapid decay of the social infrastructure, the general demoralization of the population, and the productive apathy from people refusing to work for wages that cannot sustain them will leave Jamaica too far behind the global development agenda for there any realistic hope of a speedy recovery.

[19.] Seaga, Edward, Presentation to Parliament, October 9, 2012
[20.] Clinton, Bill, Presentation to the Democratic National Conference, September 5, 2012
[21.] Clarke, Claude, What Will Fuel our Growth, In Focus, The Sunday Gleaner, August 24, 2014

In an obvious caution to the government, the *Jamaica Observer* of Sunday, November 9, 2014, published an editorial entitled "Again, Austerity Will Not Bring Economic Growth!" It summed up the 2013 commentaries by three policymakers on the merit of raising taxes and cutting public spending as the core method of economic stabilization as follows:

> The first concludes that austerity is a dangerous idea, the second says austerity kills, and the third speaks of austerity as the great failure. Economists are now recognising that austerity is neither necessary nor sufficient for economic recovery.[22]

The administration should have found a better balance between the social and economic poles. The burden of the macroeconomic fix should also have been spread more evenly across the economic strata. Instead, the economic programme has resulted in the widening of the income disparity and the wealth gap. The JLP-led administration of 2007–11 and the current PNP government should have rejected "record profits" in a shrinking economy, especially where those profits were being made, through the public debt, from the direct economic oppression of the general population and the decimation of Jamaica's current and future prospects. Austerity is both bad economics and bad politics. There are few austerity success stories and even fewer austerity administrations that survive ensuing elections.

Because of this systemic and abiding economic suppression of the Jamaican masses, the idea of independence has not resulted in real independence for too many Jamaicans. Too many persons are dependent on PATH welfare, political patronage, and other types of handouts; and too many women, girls, and young males have been forced by the prevailing conditions into economic sex slavery. Too many persons are deprived of the freedom of movement and upward social mobility, because there are still too many restrictions on progress, too many gangs and garrisons, too many curfews, and too few opportunities for the people. Too many Jamaicans have been trapped in an intergenerational downward spiral of poverty because economic recovery and prosperity *cannot* be constructed on social injustice, and a society that restricts the progress of the greater mass of its people must fail.

> Economic recovery and prosperity *cannot* be constructed on social injustice and a society which restricts the progress of the greater mass of its people must fail.

First, it was the horrendous slave labour; then it was the punishing working hours, under dreadful working conditions, for incredibly low wages. Now it is the oppressive taxation, exorbitant commodity and service charges, and a crippling public debt. Through the public debt stock alone, 43 percent of the people's money and what can yet be borrowed on their behalf is funneled into the profits of the already-rich. The exploitation does not end there. After all this, the people still have to contend with high bank charges and interest rates, excessive professional service charges, some of the highest electricity costs in the world, and when the exchange rate of the dying Jamaican dollar is factored, some of the lowest wages in the western hemisphere. The fact that so many persons still manage to squeeze survival out of the national economic obstacle course they face day after day, year after year, is testimony to the sheer strength, frugality, and tenacity of the Jamaican people—especially the womenfolk.

[22.] Editorial, the *Jamaica Observer*, November 11, 2014

It is always the regular Jamaican people who have to bear the bulk of the burden for the perennial structural adjustments and pick up the tabs for the repetitive economic fixes. They carried the burdens of the well-needed social transformation in the mid-1970s and the subsequent structural adjustments, which were compounded by the rapid increases in oil prices and the "tighter than a sardine tin" economic sabotage in the late 1970s. The people were instructed to "bite the bullet" of the punishing austerity measures of the mid-1980s. The population suffered the cost of the high-interest debt burden occasioned by the financial sector crash of the mid-1990s, and it is the poor and working class who are once again being subjected to the cruelty of the current crushing macroeconomic fix.

> But the truth, the harsh truth, is that far too few have benefitted far too much, for far too long, from the sacrifices of far too many.

There is a major economic meltdown in Jamaica every decade since the 1970s, and every time it occurs, the development of the country is set back by many years. This latest round of economic crisis began in 2008, and full seven years later, there is still no end in sight. How long must the Jamaican people suffer? When will the oppressive cycle end?

The social elite walk away scot free every time. They do not have to suspend their ambitions or even adjust their lifestyles. In fact, they get even richer. But the truth, the harsh truth, is that far too few have benefitted far too much, for far too long, from the sacrifices of far too many. The common mass of people has nothing left to ransom to the wealthy. Whenever that happens, something else will have to give. However, Robotham is correct. Hope exists. The pandemonium can still be averted. "There is still time, but not much."[23]

Abraham Lincoln's caution is that "you can fool some of the people all of the time, and all of the people some of the time, but you cannot fool all of the people all of the time." Surely, the poignant questions that must indeed be asked are, *Will we, as a people, face the facts? Will our leadership rise to the challenge? Or will the facts eventually overtake us all?*

[23.] Robotham, Don, Jamaica on the Brink, In Focus, the *Sunday Gleaner*, October 21, 2012

CHAPTER FOUR

THE VOTE AND THE VOICE

Whenever a successful case for constitutional reform has been made, the follow-up questions, which might remain, will quite likely relate to content and process. These are questions of what to reform and how to effect those reforms. Naturally, determinations have to be made about the defects and deficiencies in the existing constitution, after which, these must be related to the desired directions and destination of the society and economy.

Following on Norman Manley's formulation about the purpose of a constitution, the first consideration of constitutional reform is a framework for good governance. This broadly encompasses a discourse about citizenship, the structure of government, the administration of justice, public finances, public service, and public accountability. This discussion will be confined in a targeted manner to governance, citizenship, justice, and public accountability as well as social and economic justice issues.

PARLIAMENTARY DEMOCRACY VERSUS REPUBLICANISM

The obvious alternative route to the grant of independence would have been revolution—and it could still be. Britain was no stranger to revolution. Britain's North American colony, which became the United States of America, had successfully chosen that route to self-determination between 1774 and 1783. Revolutions tend to result in a more radical transformation of the social structures within repressive and autocratic societies. The grant of independence, despite the best hopes of the advocates, often derails the dream of personal self-determination for the broad mass of respective populations. The grant of independence has resulted in the postponement of the aspirations of equality of opportunities for the average Jamaican citizen. It has given the people their own government, but it has not substantially changed their social and economic conditions.

Freedom, independence, and justice are existentially transcendental. No one can "grant" them because they should not have been denied in the first place. They are human birthrights that are inherent in human freewill. People who are oppressed cannot wait around for some benefactor to grant them these rights. They must be claimed and asserted. Indeed, "these truths [are] self-evident, that all men are created equal, that they are endowed by their Creator with certain unalienable Rights, that among these are Life, Liberty, and the pursuit of Happiness." It is "to secure these rights

[that] Governments are instituted among Men."[1] By this declaration, governments are rendered redundant, which cannot reasonably secure the equality, liberty, security, and contentment of the greater majority of their citizens.

PARLIAMENTARY DEMOCRACY

The British parliamentary democracy evolved over a millennium and is deeply rooted in the cultural and political history of the British people. It is indigenous to Britain. At its naked core, it is a clever political scheme that preserves the prestige of the monarchy and the aristocracy while seeking to avert the violent revolution against aristocratic rule by the mass of its people—as was witnessed from close quarters across the English Channel in the French Revolution of 1789 to 1799. Parliamentary democracy gave the vote to the people, but it did not significantly change the economic and social class arrangements within the British Empire. Parliamentary democracy has had the identical effect on Jamaica.

Since independence, Jamaica has been quixotically attempting—but failing miserably—to establish equality in a political framework that does not support equality, but is built on the basic infrastructure of the House of Lords and the House of Commons. All men are not created equal in parliamentary democracy governance systems. There is a basic, perhaps unwitting, underlying presumption that there are "lords" and there are "commoners," and "masters" and "servants" in the parliamentary democracy system and in the societies in which they are promulgated. That is the primary reason the democratic socialist experiment of the 1970s crashed so miserably. Equal rights cannot be pursued in a governance system and within a social mind-set that do not intrinsically support social justice and the equitable pursuit of life, liberty, and happiness.

FIGURE 6: THE PARLIAMENTARY HYBRID

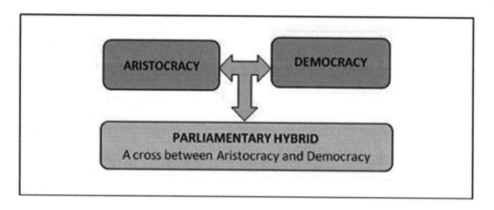

The parliamentary democracy system of government developed from the autocratic belief that "everyone is born equal, but some are born more equal than others" and possess the inherent birthright to a "right of passage" and the power to make determinations on behalf of all others without consulting them. It is arguably the same perception that gave rise to slavery, and it continues to perpetuate the exploitation of the masses. Genuine democracy is founded on a fundamental belief

---

[1.] From the US Declaration of Independence document

28

in the equality of all citizens and their equal participation in the decision-making process. Authentic democracy is consultative governance by all the citizens of the state.

FIGURE 7: THE REPUBLICAN MODEL

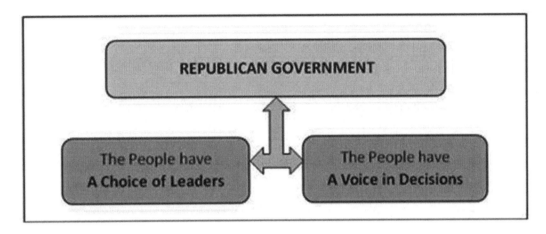

The parliamentary hybrid is therefore a cross between aristocracy and democracy. It is not a full democracy. It proposes equality but maintains an aristocratic class. It grants the people a choice of the leaders who govern them, but it does not always give the people a voice in the decisions that are made on their behalf. Real democracy gives both vote and voice. It is important to note that in countries where there is no formalized aristocracy, parliamentary democracy often creates a substitute aristocratic class from elected and appointed representatives and the descendants of the dominant colonial class.

TABLE 3: REPUBLICANISM VS. PARLIAMENTARY DEMOCRACY

Parliamentary Hybrid	Republicanism
▪ Preserves aristocratic hegemony	▪ Entrenches the *equality* of all persons
▪ Exchanges the old aristocracy for an "elected aristocracy" and maintains class structures	▪ Eliminates all forms of aristocracy and segregation, including "elected aristocrats"
▪ Places too much power in the hands of the "elected aristocracy"	▪ Exposes all critical public officials to entrenched systems of *accountability*
▪ Limits systems of public accountability on public officers	▪ Enforces accountability for all public officers through administrative checks and balances
▪ Struggles with attempts to expand systems of accountability since it was *not* formulated on the premise of public accountability	▪ Establishes the basis for the separation of powers and greater accountability of the executive to parliament and the people
▪ Limits the people's participation in public affairs beyond the election of leaders	▪ Expands opportunities of all citizens for *participation* in the way they are governed
▪ Limits people participation by centralizing the governance structures	▪ Ensures *people self-determination* and *responsibility* though local government

Republic literally means "re" the "public," therefore republicanism is "government in reference to the public." Republicans maintain that democratic governance is not a private or family affair; governance is a public matter. This means that essential public offices must be filled through democratic elections, and important public decisions must be decided democratically in a public manner. Parliamentary democracy cedes public decision making to elected officials, who are more often than not more influenced by powerful, private interest caucuses than what is good for the general population. Republicanism is often a slow and tedious process, but it proposes to give both the choice to the people as to who leads and a voice in the decisions that are made on their behalf. The central concerns of republicanism are therefore equality, democracy, and accountability.

THE PARLIAMENTARY FAÇADE

Parliamentary democracy is not built on the principle of equality and struggles with economic and social reform efforts that are designed to create greater opportunities for the broader mass of the population. In order to achieve the preservation of class divides, parliamentary democracy operates as a political smokescreen, creating the illusion of people power by shifting governments. Each time the economic and social tensions reach boiling point, a new government is elected. This gives the illusion that "the people have spoken," but the oppressive social structures persist, undisturbed by the election of a new administration. In republicanism, the people maintain their voice and can demand change, even without changing governments. In the parliamentary hybrid, progress can only result from the goodwill of a progressive leadership core. However, governance cannot be left to goodwill. Independence is for self-determination, and only republicanism can ensure political self-determination.

The idea of a republic is therefore more far-reaching than the mere sentimentality of removing the monarchy. It incorporates the considerations about the extension of equality, the widening of democratic power, making leaders more accountable, and giving more political power to the people. Republicanism is ultimately about the advancement and acceleration of national development in the equitable interest of *all* the citizens.

LOCAL EMPOWERMENT VERSUS POLITICAL CENTRISM

Republicanism is closely related to community self-determination and community self-reliance. Michael Manley remarked that Jamaica's local government system is perhaps the only one in the world in which there is "responsibility without power." It was his observation that after the citizens undertake the periodic "charade of electing a local government authority," that authority can do nothing without the expressed permission of a centralized department of local government. Consequently, "power resides ultimately at the center." Manley believed that this anomaly in Jamaica's governance structure was a colonial legacy that has been perpetuated by a constitutional oversight.[2] This continues to be a major weakness in the Jamaican governance structure.

Local government is the foundation of the overall governance framework. Sustainable national development *cannot* be achieved without a resourceful local government system. Consequently, it is

---

[2.]   Manley, Politics of Change: 72

not surprising that most developed societies boast autonomous local government authorities. This is quite understandable since "the people of an area must be encouraged to think for themselves and come up with ideas for their own development, which can be subsequently refined and rendered feasible by centrally located technicians."[3]

Among the admirable reform objectives that the Ministry of Local Government and Community Development has outlined are the following:

1. To entrench local government in the constitution of Jamaica.
2. To recognize local government as a separate and autonomous sphere of government through the allocation of functions best administered and regulated at the local level.
3. To guarantee the security (predictability and sufficiency through central government transfer) of financial resources for local authorities and the increased contribution of independent sources of their own income.
4. To provide a modern legal framework for the viable operation of local authorities, including the authority to conduct the functions and responsibilities assigned; the delineation of the scope and power of mayors, councillors, and secretary managers; the financing of local authorities; and the management of their human resources.[4]

With the one exception of local authorities depending upon central government for resources, these changes are critical for Jamaica's advancement. However, these impressive proposals have been pending for well over two decades and more than forty years since Michael Manley first called attention to the glaring deficiencies in local government. If succeeding governments have been convinced about the potential of local government to advance national development, why have the political leaders fumbled the changes for so long? Constitutional reform efforts should have addressed these issues expeditiously.

If Jamaica's communities are to finally realize the goal of independence and self-determination, local government reforms must be effected with dispatch. In the final analysis, permitted the latitude, communities are more likely to better understand their local needs and solutions than external agencies. However, the elected aristocracy of the parliamentary hybrid cannot stomach this type of divestment of power to the people. That is the real reason local government reform has been repeatedly stalled.

In 2012, the mayor of the Kingston and St Andrew Corporation, Angela Brown-Burke, stated that it was her belief that a greater involvement of local authorities in the tax collection processes, however limited, can significantly increase revenue collection.[5] This is just one example of the potential that the empowerment of local government holds for national development. Undoubtedly, effective local government reform could also reduce the pervasive, debilitating, and potentially disruptive community-dependency syndrome and eventually lead to enhanced community development.

This approach would effectively free central government from micromanagement concerns, such as responding to road blocks and demonstrations for community social services, thereby creating

---

[3] Ibid.
[4] Ministry of Local Government and Community Development, Local Government Reform
[5] 'Smile Jamaica' Interview, October 2012

much greater scope for more focus on macrodevelopment considerations. It is entirely foolhardy, in the complexity of a modern, globalized economy, to have a critical economic minister—of say, finance, industry, tourism, or agriculture, who is also a member of parliament—bogged down with minor, rural community representational concerns when the major challenges facing Jamaica are macroeconomic issues. Ministers should be freed from such matters to be able to aggressively seek out national economic opportunities wherever they may exist across the globe.

Similarly, it is completely nonsensical for mayors and councillors to be able to proffer the excuse that town roads cannot be repaired because the roads "belong to the National Works Agency," or that they have no control over garbage collection in their own divisions because garbage collection is the exclusive remit of the National Solid Waste Authority. Something is radically wrong with this kind of frustrating governance arrangement.

Evidently, in any new arrangement, parish councillors should be required to exercise greater responsibility for their respective geographic areas, and members of parliament should be granted more latitude to concentrate on their law-making functions. They could meet more frequently and provide closer and more effective oversight over the administrative branches of government through an expanded and more formalized parliamentary committee system. This holds significant prospects for the reduction of public corruption through the approval of budgets of expenditure, the monitoring of the awards of contracts, the supervision of national development projects, and the taking of reports.

TOO MUCH GOVERNMENT

The constant economic strictures have led some political commentators to call for a reduction in the size of the cabinet. It is certainly true that Jamaica has too much government. However, Jamaica cannot successfully resolve its innumerable challenges with a small executive. It is not the cabinet that is too large, it is the parliament. Jamaica has too many members of parliament. The state of New York, for example, with a population of nineteen million has twenty-seven representatives in the US Congress, at a rate of above 1:700,000. The United States of America has 435 members of Congress for over 308 million citizens, at a rate of over 1:700,000. Jamaica has 63 members of parliament at an average rate of 1:43,000; some with much less. Each representative in the US Congress has an average of over 650,000 more constituents than the Jamaican MP. There can be no attempt to justify this massive representational disproportion without making the administrations look regressive and the parliamentarians incompetent.

> Political representation is for empowerment; not enslavement. Therefore, elected representatives are not to be measured by the volume of handouts they distribute but by the rate of development they accomplish.

Jamaica does not need more than forty-five members of parliaments—if so many—and fourteen elected senators at a rate of one per parish. If they are elected on professional competence and people commitment, rather than on a party basis, there is also no need for more than three parish councillors per constituency or a total of 135, with 14 popularly elected majors. Consider the significant annual saving to the nation in remuneration, the cost of support systems, and other benefits not paid. That is money that could go directly into community development efforts and the general economic advancement of the people.

If the members of parliament are going to be saddled with micro community representational issues, then there is absolutely no need for councillors. If the councillors, however, are to be empowered as the people's local representatives, as they ought to be, then there is no need for so many MPs. Jamaica's bloated, supersize government is a direct consequence of the unprogressive and undemocratic centralization of power inherent in the colonial mind-set of the Westminster system. It has been made far worse in Jamaica's exaggerated and backward backra-massa social configuration and operates primarily on the same colonial begging-handout-dependency system and plantation-turn-garrison control mentality, which undermine personal freedom, community independence, genuine democracy, and national development.

It is full time for Jamaica to get its political bearings right. MPs are lawmakers, and parliament is a watchdog over the administration. MPs are national legislators, not community social workers. MPs are to make laws, see that those laws are executed with dispatch, and ensure there is no corruption. It is the parish councillors who are community leaders. They are the ones who should be empowered to address community concerns. However, councillors are not welfare officers. They are the paid economic and social empowerment agents of the people. Their primary business is to help stimulate local business enterprises and make their communities harmonious and prosperous.

Political representation is for empowerment, not enslavement. Therefore, elected representatives are not to be measured by the volume of handouts they distribute but by the rate of development they accomplish. They should not be applauded for how many persons they put on welfare, but for how many persons they take off welfare. No government should take any pride in the announcement of the expansion of welfare programmes, such as an increase in the number of PATH beneficiaries. When a country makes more poor people, it is a national embarrassment, not an achievement. MPs are to make laws to grow the economy and make their country peaceful and productive. When peace is not attained and growth is not realized, they have failed.

Therefore, these questions still have to be asked: *Why then has local government reform taken so long? What are the reasons why this critical process of social and economic transformation has been postponed? Who really benefits from the delay?*

CHAPTER FIVE

REFORMATION AND SOCIAL JUSTICE

According to Norman Manley, the second major constitutional concern relates to the framework for the protection of the rights of the people. In essence, this encompasses considerations about citizenship, fundamental rights, and freedoms as well as the administration of justice.

CITIZENSHIP

Constitutional justice begins with the definition of citizenship. Jamaica's constitutional provisions for citizenship compare favourably with international standards. Section 3 of the constitution outlines that citizenship may be acquired by birth, descent, or marriage. Others can acquire citizenship through a process of naturalization, which Section 3(2) facilitates by granting the latitude to parliament to make such provisions.

Reviews about Jamaica's relationship with the queen will raise questions about the country's place in the British Commonwealth and will have ramifications for Sections 9, 10, and 12, which accord certain rights to Commonwealth citizens. Of greater concern, however, is the manner in which any new constitution will treat Jamaicans in the diaspora. The recommendation here is that all individuals who can be regarded as citizens of Jamaica by means of birth, descent, marriage, or the process of naturalization should be regarded as full Jamaican citizens, regardless of place of residence, unless by due legal process they choose to renounce that right. Exceptions will of course have to be made for the election or appointment to sensitive public offices.

THE CHARTER OF RIGHTS

The 2011 Charter of Rights is quite comprehensive in scope. Section 13(1)(c) also provides for enforceability of the rights against private persons. However, the charter runs contrary to international trends with regard to the inherent rights of the individual as a human being in relation to the right to life, the freedom from cruel and inhumane treatment, and freedom from all forms of discrimination. The fundamental rights and freedoms are also limited by the savings clause of Section 13(7). A new constitution must make a definitive determination on the legal landscape going forward and abolish all saving clauses from the constitution.

Justifications for inhumane treatment have no place in a modern charter of rights, and a country which has to resort to such backwardness is in a dark and desperate place.

Section 13(8) preserves the death penalty, regardless of the duration of incarceration or the conditions under which death row prisoners are held. This was cleverly included to counter the UKPC's ruling in *Pratt and Morgan* that if the time that elapsed between the sentence of death and execution exceeds five years, "there will be strong grounds for believing that the delay was such as to constitute inhumane or degrading punishment or other treatment."[1] However, this provision runs contrary to the general directions in international law regarding the abolition of capital punishment and represents an offence to the spirit of "rights and freedoms."

Rationalizations for the retention of capital punishment may, however, be rooted in the belief that the law must reflect the general mores of the society. Oliver Wendell Holmes Jr. noted that "the law embodies the story of a nation's development through many centuries."[2] Hanging is a part of Jamaica's colonial legacy. It was utilized by the planters to contain revolts against slavery and colonial oppression and to safeguard their economic interests. It is the brazen and ubiquitous economic exploitation of the common mass of people that robs the nation and its people of the resources for advancement, and at the baseline, it is this exploitation that fuels Jamaica's high murder rate. It is the same colonial mentality and the passive acceptance of the prevailing inequitable economic equations by the people that keep the noose hanging around the necks of the general population. Some of Jamaica's economic elites still do not think of murders in terms of lives lost and the associated emotional pain and suffering; their primary concern is often about how their business is affected and its impact on their economic fortunes.

The resolution to the high murder rate will not be found in more deaths through hanging and more repression of the people. Repression is the *modus operandi* of the exploiter. Those who are genuinely interested in the development of the people usually concentrate their efforts on finding the ways and means to expand the opportunities for more persons to be lifted from the frustrating conditions that breed violence. In the end, constitutions—and charters of rights even more so—are to be formulated on quality of life issues. Justifications for inhumane treatment have no place in a modern charter of rights and a country that has to resort to such backwardness is in a dark and desperate place, rushing to recourse to a scourge that most advancing societies have abolished.

CITIZENS' CHARTER

The rights of the citizen are outlined in the constitution, and breaches of these rights and freedoms are actionable before the courts. The question of the responsibilities of the citizen to the state must also be enshrined within the constitution, and breaches must become actionable by the state. They must also carry appropriate sanctions.

Chapter 4 of the constitution of New Zealand contains a citizens' charter (appendix 2) that sets out the duties and responsibilities of the citizens. It represents a good basis on which a Jamaican citizen's charter can be formulated. In addition to the clauses contained therein, in light of pervasive national challenges, a Jamaican citizen's charter should also demand the following:

1. The positive duty of patriotism: to respect national symbols, to defend Jamaica, and to protect public institutions.

[1.] Pratt and Morgan v. Attorney General for Jamaica, [1993] 1 UKPC 1
[2.] Holmes, Oliver Wendell, Jr., 1897. The Path of the Law, Harvard Law Review 10 (March): 457–461. 1963

2. The duty to participate in the economic life of the country: to pay the appropriate taxes as established by the Parliament and to maintain a productive life.
3. The duty to make a positive contribution to the social development of the country: to provide a safe and loving home and community environment, to provide reasonable care for children and dependents, to assist the vulnerable; and to respect the rights of others.
4. The duty to live ethically and responsibly: to resist and report corruption, to contribute reasonably to crime-fighting efforts and the maintenance of public order.
5. The duty to participate in the political life of the country: to remain reasonably appraised of national and community issues and to vote their consciences.
6. The duty to participate in the development of the local community.
7. The duty to protect and preserve the natural environment.

One of the challenges with the constitution is that some critical provisions are not generally known by the citizens that they are designed to bind or protect, and they are not backed up by enforcing legislative, administrative, prosecutorial, or judicial mechanisms. In order for these patriotic duties to take full effect, the citizen's charter should also contain a provision that requires the state to take reasonable steps to consistently promote these duties among the general population, particularly in educational institutions. They should in fact be included in the schools' curriculum. The citizens should be taught their rights as well as their responsibilities.

THE ADMINISTRATION OF JUSTICE

The administration of justice occupied a central place in the formulation of the 1962 Constitution. Norman Manley admitted that the final product regarding this important component required "deliberate acts of compromise by many persons."[3] The three towers of justice, which resulted from the deliberations, were the following:

1. In Section 94, the office of the director of Public Prosecution, which has jurisdiction over all criminal prosecutions and is constitutionally protected from political interference;
2. In Section 98, the office of the chief justice, as the head of the judicial system, with the occupier of the office having the right to sit in the Court of Appeal, and the only judge who has the right to sit at both levels of the judiciary;
3. In Section 120, the office of the attorney general, the occupier being the "guardian of criminal law . . . and the potential guardian of the public against the encroachment of civil authority, he must see that justice is done."[4] The attorney general is also the chief legal counsel to the government.

The novel justice related inclusion in the 1962 Constitution was the establishment of the Court of Appeal in Section 103, with judges who, except for the chief justice, were separate and distinct from trial judges.

---

[3] Nettleford: 307–307
[4] Ibid.

THE OFFICE OF THE ATTORNEY GENERAL

Norman Manley agonized about the possibility of duplicity in the "ancient, honourable, and highly important" office of the attorney general and cautioned that the exercise of the powers in criminal matters should be free from any political interference whatsoever.[5] The question of whether the attorney general should be appointed by the government is still a vexed question, and constitutional reform should deal definitively with the separation of the "guardian of the criminal law" and "the legal advisor to the government."

Section 79(3) provides that the attorney general *is not* de facto a cabinet member. There appears to be inherent procedural contradictions where, for example, the attorney general is also the minister of justice. This was highlighted in the Manatt-Coke Commission of Enquiry. In their report, the commissioners recommended a "separation of powers" between the executive and judicial functions of the position.[6] The current administration has separated both offices but has not gone far enough. In the interest of "the appearance of justice," the attorney general should not be a government appointee or a member of parliament. The office should be constitutionally separated completely from the influence of the executive.

CORRUPTION

A second major challenge with the administration of justice in Jamaica is the prevalence of corruption. Corruption in public office is a serious criminal offence and should be treated as such. Public corruption is economic robbery with aggravation. It is a betrayal of public trust and undermines the entire governance framework. It robs the country of scarce resources and is a capital assault on the collective progress and prospects of the young people of the nation. It should attract serious criminal sanctions.

> Public corruption is economic robbery with aggravation. It is a betrayal of public trust and undermines the entire governance framework.

The main deficiency in the prevention of corruption is the paucity of the mechanisms for effective investigation and successful prosecution of the perversion of established procedural standards and fiduciary responsibility. Corruption represents such a serious threat to Jamaica's progress and causes such a drain on public resources that it should be regarded as an urgent national priority that must attract the requisite focus at the constitutional level to bring about swift and effective containment and resolution.

Former Prime Minister Bruce Golding had proposed a special prosecutor, and former Contractor General Greg Christie proposed a single anticorruption agency. When these proposals are pursued to their natural conclusion, it becomes clear that the modern governance structure is in need of a "fourth pillar of government" to police the conduct of the administration and to facilitate the administration of justice. The various components of this fourth pillar of government already exist, and a fusing and formalizing of the structures are likely to result in greater efficiency and represent less strain on the national purse over the long term. It should be quite obvious to those who are seeking to remedy these deficiencies in the legal system that the administration of justice is a major

---

5.   Ibid.
6.   Report of the Commission of Enquiry, into the Extradition Request for Christopher Coke: 56

plank upon which the constitution is formulated. Any attempt to plug these gaps without grounding them in the constitution will not go far enough. It is from the constitution that justice draws it efficacy.

The office of the attorney general, the office of the contractor general, the office of the auditor general, the public defender, the proposed office of the special prosecutor, the Human Rights Commission, the Integrity Commission, IDECOM, the corruption prevention agencies, the ombudsmen, and all other similar watchdog organs might quite properly be located within the fourth pillar of government. This constitutional pillar should quite naturally be headed by a genuinely independent attorney general, whose primary obligation would be to see that social and economic justice is always done. The efficiency and effectiveness of a fourth branch of government would necessitate skilled and committed investigative capabilities and case management systems for rapid resolution. Corruption justice ought to be swift, decisive, and definitive if it is to be effective.

JUSTICE DELAYED

From a practical point of view, the foremost concerns with the justice system are the inadequate access to, and the sluggish pace of, justice in Jamaica. It has been often said that "justice delayed is justice denied." If this is true, then there is very limited justice in Jamaica.

In 2007, the Justice System Reform Task Force indicated in their comprehensive 319-page final report that the major problems with the justice system were

1. the slow pace of the court system,
2. the cost of dispute resolution in the courts,
3. limited public understanding of the work of the courts and the system as a whole, and
4. lack of public confidence in the system.[7]

The task force also found that the justice system is

i. too unequal: there is a lack of equality between the powerful, wealthy litigant and the under-resourced litigant.
ii. too expensive: the costs often exceed the value of the claim, and also some ways of proceeding are cost-ineffective from the perspective of the justice system.
iii. too uncertain: the difficulty of forecasting what litigation will cost and how long it will last, induces fear of the unknown, and there is also a lack of consistency in outcomes.
iv. too slow in bringing cases to a conclusion.
v. too complicated: both the law and procedure can be incomprehensible for many people.
vi. too fragmented in the way it is organized: there is no one with clear overall responsibility for the administration of justice.
vii. too adversarial: while proceedings must respect the adversarial process, there is room for cooperation to make proceedings and the system more efficient.[8]

[7.] Justice System Reform Task Force, Final Report, 2007:15
[8.] Ibid. 14–15

The task force proposed that reform should be guided by the vision statement: The Jamaican justice system is available, accessible, accountable, and affordable on a timely, courteous, respectful, flexible, fair, and competent basis for all.[9]

Notwithstanding the extensive list of pragmatic recommendations that is contained in the report, the administration of justice is first and foremost a creature of the constitution. Despite his characteristic professional graciousness at the time, it was quite unambiguous from Norman Manley's comments on the extensive compromises surrounding the 1962 constitutional provisions regarding the administration of justice, that he felt then, that Jamaica had not received the optimum construct for a dependable justice system. There is the distinct possibility that he would have sought to amend the constitution had he been elected to lead the government after independence. The demands on the system are far more complex and comprehensive more than fifty years on.

At the very least, common sense suggests a review of the constitutional provisions for the justice system. The formalization of the office of special prosecutor, for example, cannot be achieved without alterations to an entrenched constitutional provision. Section 94(3)(a), 3(b) and 3(c) of the constitution gives the director of public prosecution the jurisdiction to initiate, take over, or discontinue criminal charges. Those powers remain outside the scope of legislation. This is essentially true for most of the progressive legal changes that Jamaica urgently requires. It is virtually impossible to construct a sturdy governance structure on a faulty, shaky, colonial constitutional foundation, which had too many compromises from the start and which has evidently become time-worn. The establishment of a single anticorruption branch without a special prosecutor with constitutional authority to initiate, take over, or discontinue corruption charges against agents and agencies of the state will be a glorious exercise in futility and another smokescreen of progress; and to achieve that office, the constitution has to be amended.

> It is virtually impossible to construct a sturdy governance structure on a faulty, shaky, colonial constitutional foundation, which had too many compromises from the start and which has evidently become time-worn.

In the final analysis, however, court efficiency is often tied to the adequacy of funding. Gleaner columnist and attorney-at-law Gordon Robinson has raised the issue of dedicated, independent funding for the judiciary.[10] In addition to the court fines Robinson has advanced, a similar funding arrangement to the CCJ could also be adapted into the Jamaican justice system and expanded to address the infrastructure and general resource needs of the court system. If the country could have raised US$28.7 million to fund a regional court, which it might never fully utilize, it ought to be able to find the resources to make its own national court system truly independent and efficient. This is a particularly critical consideration in light of Jamaica's persistently high crime rate because there will be no peace until there is justice.

---

9.   Ibid. 17
10.   Robinson, Gordon, My Vote of No Confidence, In Focus, the *Sunday Gleaner*, November 23, 2014

THE CARIBBEAN COURT OF JUSTICE

No study on constitutional reform of Jamaica's justice system is complete without a discussion on the Caribbean Court of Justice, CCJ. The CCJ has been advanced over many years as a constitutional sticking point between Jamaica's two major political parties. It continues to muddy the constitutional reform conversation. The UKHL has ruled in *IJCHR v Syringa Marshall-Burnett,* Privy Council Appeal No. 41 of 2004, that a referendum is required for Jamaica to accede to the appellate jurisdiction of the CCJ.

> If the CCJ continues to have that "red herring effect," it should be taken off the constitutional reform agenda. The justice of expanded social opportunities and economic prosperity far surpasses all other justice concerns.

Guyana, Barbados, and Belize already have the CCJ as their final appeals court. Dominica also acceded on July 1, 2014, by way of a letter of assent from the British government and a subsequent two-thirds majority vote in the Dominican Parliament, with eighteen yeas to three abstentions.[11] So Jamaica, the former champion of legal and political innovation in the Caribbean Region, has, out of political expediency, become the most constitutionally regressive. With the UK facing its own challenges, one can only hope that Jamaica will not remain a "hanger on" to the UKPC until it has been forcibly evicted. The pursuit of independence requires taking charge of one's own affairs, or at the very minimum, it anticipates equal partnerships.

Although the full adoption of the CCJ should have been set within the context of comprehensive constitutional reforms instead of constitutional incrementalism, there can be no reasonable claim to independence with a foreign head of state and a final court in a distant metropolis, outside of the reach of the vast majority of the country's citizens. There is no independence when the legislature, the executive, and the judiciary are tied in subservience to foreign powers. After more than fifty years of talking independence, all three branches of Jamaica's government have remained colonially fettered. After more than fifty years of talking economic advancement, Jamaica's duly elected government is still at the economic and political mercy of external lending agencies and local private interest groups.

In light of Jamaica's pressing social and economic challenges, if the CCJ continues to have that "red herring effect," it should be taken off the constitutional reform agenda. The justice of expanded social opportunities and economic prosperity far surpasses all other justice concerns. In the final analysis, however, as eminent international jurist, Jamaican Judge Patrick Robinson has reminded, "It is better to misgovern one's self than to be governed by someone else."[12] In any event, there are very few Jamaicans who can in fact afford access to the UKPC, and some might not even qualify for a visa to enter the UK. Therefore those who oppose the CCJ as final court are effectively thwarting Jamaica's independence and denying Jamaicans of justice.

---

11.   Douglas, Eisenhower, Sovereignty, Independence and the Caribbean Court of Justice, Dominica News Online
12.   Meikle, Ashford W., *Is the CCJ a Trojan Horse?* Sunday Gleaner, December 26, 2010

OTHER JUSTICE AND ADMINISTRATIVE CONSIDERATIONS

HEAD OF STATE

The two major political parties have already locked horns with each other over the issue of the head of state. They both agree that there should be an elected head and a ceremonial head, but they cannot agree on what to name which. They are both wrong, and they are wrong because they cannot seem to break free of the mind-set of the colonial aristocracy in which some representatives appear so tightly cloaked.

First of all, a "republican parliamentary democracy" is a classic political oxymoron, and the political leaders need to begin to think outside of that box. Secondly, if a country elects its national leader on a popular ballot, there is no need, beyond colonial sentimentality, for a ceremonial head of state. The ceremonial head of state of the parliamentary democracy was designed to preserve the prestige of, and give relevance to, the monarchy. The United States of America, with over three hundred million citizens and the largest economy in the world, has flourished without a ceremonial head of state. There are many other large, progressive countries without monarchs or ceremonial heads.

Jamaica does not need two political heads. One is more than sufficient. That would immediately release about thirty police officers who are currently assigned to the protection of the governor general. That is more than many police stations have for the protection of thousands of citizens. It would also free up a significant portion of the budget, as well as King House and acres of prime city land—perhaps to build a modern parliament building. If real progress is ever to be realized, the nation's political leaders and administration must speedily shake off the penchant to expand, complicate, and slow down government and replace it with a consuming desire for efficiency and effectiveness.

There is an urgent need for an emancipation from colonial nostalgia and administrative bureaucracy in Jamaican politics. The country has struggled so hard to advance because too many of its leaders are stuck in a colonial time warp with wigs, robes, and titles and relics such as the "Throne Speech," "Kings House," "Queen's Counsels," and all. The country will never be able to move forward with so many of its leaders fighting so hard to retain the fetters of pre-independence aristocratic prestige.

It is little wonder then that class exploitation is so rampant. Too many of the elected and appointed aristocrats cannot see it let alone correct it. Some even appear quite comfortable with it and are even prepared to openly ridicule colleagues who seek to speak up for the poor. What is even more disheartening is that in a country with so many poor people, they are allowed to get away with it. However, after so many years of being held hostage to pervasive class oppression, Stockholm syndrome has set in, and the electorate has also become accommodating of class divides and blinded to its evils.

REPUBLICAN GOVERNMENT, RECALL AND TERM LIMITS

The Jamaican population has indicated that it is ready to elect its prime minister on a popular ballot rather than to have their national leader selected by political party delegates. The *Gleaner*-commissioned Bill Johnson poll published on Friday, October 17, 2014, revealed that "[e]ighty per cent of Jamaicans want to vote directly for their prime minister."[13] The same series of polls showed that 82 percent of the population also wants constitutional amendments "to allow voters to recall non-performing members of parliament (MPs)."[14]

Except for blind party hacks, "all politics is economics" and the parliamentary system of government was originally designed to pit the representatives of the aristocracy against the representatives of the "commoners." This was certainly true in Jamaica where the advocates of "the common mass of the people" found themselves in a sudden and unexpected electoral contest with the political proxies of the ruling class in 1944. This political battle of the classes reached fever pitch in the late 1970s because Michael Manley and his government were audacious enough to raise the economic scale of the poor and upset the colonial wealth and opportunity imbalance.

> There are still too many Jamaicans who have not grasped the economics in Jamaican politics and it is this ignorance that continues to feed wealth transfer and economic stagnation.

The ongoing political clash of economic interests has created deep divisions in the political system and the society—not the least of which is garrison politics. There are still too many Jamaicans, even among the educated professionals, who have not grasped the economic dynamics in Jamaican politics, and it is this ignorance that continues to perpetuate exploitation, feed wealth transfer, and breed economic stagnation. It is time for the people to stop fighting for parties and begin to fight for progress.

For over fifty years, the citizens have been forced by the divide-and-rule Westminster parliamentary tribal democracy to split into hostile opponents along party lines every five years to defend their real or perceived political interests. The popular election of the prime minister can create the scope for reduced political tensions and the broadening of democracy as it would provide more latitude for the electorate to vote their consciences. Voters would no longer feel obligated to elect or vote out any MP, regardless of his or her competence, simply because they want a particular party to form the government.

If the election of the legislators is separated from the election of the prime minister, electors could choose to vote for individual MPs, regardless of political party, and still get the executive of their choice. They could vote for independents, third parties, and even candidates from opposing parties and still retain their choice of prime minister and administration. It takes no stretch of the imagination to grasp the prospects that such a political structure holds for the democratization and maturity of Jamaica's political processes.

An indigenous and ingenious Jamaican republican system of government could also aid in lessening political polarization and tribalism, reduce the continuous campaigning, the "clashing of political titans" and the constant "oppose, oppose, oppose" by abolishing the post of Leader of Opposition and replacing it with Minority and Majority Leaders in the House of Representatives. Where there are more than two parties, all the minority leaders of political parties represented in parliament could be granted similar procedural deference now accorded to the leader of the opposition in parliament.

---

[13]. J'cans Want Direct Vote for PM, the *Gleaner*, Friday, October 17, 2014
[14]. Ibid.

Clearly, too, Jamaican republicanism and local government reforms can be shaped to broaden democratization by breaking the political stranglehold of the PNP and JLP on the representation of the people. This can be achieved by deliberately creating more room for the inclusion of other political movements and independents. This perspective appears to enjoy the support of the mayor of Black River, Everton Fisher, who has been bold enough to declare, "to deafening applause" by his audience, that "I believe strongly that Jamaica needs more than two parties . . . for too long politics has divided us and is all because of this two-party system."[15] What the mayor has probably not recognized is that it has contributed significantly to Jamaica's economic stagnation as well.

Professor Brian Meeks, director of the Sir Arthur Lewis Institute for Social and Economic Studies at the Mona campus of the University of the West Indies, has added his voice to the rising chorus for term limits on the prime ministers, albeit within the broader context of the Caribbean. He believes that prime ministers who occupy the post for too long run the risk of becoming complacent and arrogant and "begin to feel like [they] own the plantation."[16] The irony is that though it is even more appropriate for parliamentary democracies where the people have a limited choice in the selection of their prime minister; it is republicanism, where people often choose their leaders directly, that tends to impose term limits. Term limits are not necessary where political leaders are democratically elected on a popular ballot. The elected leader is the choice of the people, and the people's choice should not be restricted. However, the term limit is a useful constitutional safeguard against tyranny and electoral perversion.

THE SENATE

The Jamaican Senate is an "imitation House of Lords." Undoubtedly, the House of Lords was initially designed to give the aristocracy the powers to review laws passed by the House of Commons, or effectively, to provide legislative protection for the interests of the ruling classes. The UK Privy Council was probably originally projected to serve the same function as it relates to decisions of the courts of the colonies. Genuine efforts at democratization ought to consider a review of the purpose, structure, and composition of the country's legislative review panel.

> The senate exists to ensure that no law is passed by parliament and no action is taken by government that contravenes either the spirit or the letter of the constitutional rights of the people.

A significant number of postcolonial governments are unicameral. Serious constitutional review should make a determination on whether or not a senate is in fact needed at all and whether or not a properly resourced parliamentary counsel cannot effectively advise parliament on the legal interests of the people. At the very minimum, considerations ought to be given to the manner in which senators are chosen. Republican democracy suggests that senators should face the people at the polls. If an appointed senate is maintained, it should at least be configured to include independent or proportionally selected senators.

In the end, however, a Jamaican Senate, which is a creature of a constitution promulgated on the principles of genuine democracy, and the fundamental equality of all its citizens must be deliberately designed to provide wide representation and effective protection for the broad interests of the

---

15. Myers, Garfield, PNP Mayor Calls for Multi-party Democracy, The Jamaica Observer, December 11, 2014
16. Brian Meeks Calls for Fixed Term for Caribbean PMs, Jamaica Observer, November 29, 2014

Jamaican people. In other words, the senate should be made to understand that it exists as the primary guardian of the constitution and that as a component of government, it has one principal duty and that is to ensure that no law is passed by parliament and no action is taken by government that contravenes either the spirit or the letter of the constitutional rights of the people. It is the duty of the senate to ensure that the Jamaican society is just and equitable.

TREATY LAWS

A significant concern in treaty laws is justice. There is often a long delay between the time Jamaica ratifies a convention and the time the parliament finally passes the enacting legislation. Jamaica ratified the Convention on the Rights of Persons with Disabilities on March 31, 2007. It took seven years for the enabling bill to be passed by the pedestrian parliament. The treatment of international laws should also be reviewed. Drafting and parliamentary time and resources could be saved if a new constitution created the scope for automatic incorporation of the treaty and convention laws that Jamaica ratifies.

TABLE 4: SUMMARY OF RECOMMENDED CONSTITUTIONAL CHANGES

RECOMMENDED CONSTITUTIONAL CHANGES
Develop an indigenized republican system of government with partial separation of powers
Establish the prime minister as the Jamaican head of state
Activate provisions for the popular election of the prime minister
Create latitude for cabinet members who are not parliamentarians
Reduce the number of members of parliament to forty-five
Abolish the post of leader of the opposition and replace it with Minority/Majority Leaders
Review the number, role, and selection process of the members of the Senate
Review the role and powers of the House Speaker and the Senate President
Broaden democracy with deliberate scope for new political movements and independents
Set term limits on important public offices
Establish systems of recall for nonperforming elected public officials
Establish impeachment mechanisms for senior public offices
Create scope for automatic incorporation of treaty laws
Entrench local government with adequate funding and authority
Empower parish councils to take charge of local social and economic development
Elect all parish council heads on a popular parish ballot
Redefine *citizenship* to more clearly include all Jamaicans abroad
Include a Citizens' Charter in the constitution
Activate systems to teach constitutional rights and responsibilities to citizen
Remove the death penalty references in the Charter of Rights
Remove all saving clauses from the Jamaican legal system
Activate mechanisms to enforce critical constitutional provisions

Delink the attorney general completely from politics
Establish a Fourth Pillar (The Regulatory Branch) of government
Establish the office of the special prosecutor
Modernize the administration of justice
Establish the CCJ as Jamaica's final court

CHAPTER SIX

REFORMATION AND DEVELOPMENT

The third consideration in Norman Manley's formula for constitution writing is a consideration about "the purpose and intention in which the government stands."[1] This presumes that the government possesses a basic grasp of the country's challenges and at least a broad sketch of the developmental goals for the country. If a constitution is to contribute to the peaceful progression and the social and economic advancement of its people, certain hallmark constitutional imperatives are indispensable. These include considerations about the following:

1. Identity—through patriotic pride and a sense of nationalism
2. Unity—through patriotic commitment above personal and partisan concerns
3. Equality—through affirmative action for the expansion of opportunities for all
4. Justice—through a recalibration of skewed social and economic opportunities
5. Participation—through genuine democratization of governance structures
6. Accountability—through effective systems of checks and balances
7. Prosperity—through creativity, innovation, inclusiveness, productivity and honesty

The Jamaican Constitution should also be linguistically accessible, which is to say that it should be written in plain and simple language. It belongs to the entire population, not just the legal fraternity. It should also be so "Jamaicanized" and so contextualized that it practically "comes to life." It should speak concretely to the conditions and ambitions of the people.

IDENTITY AND UNITY

The philosophical core problem with the 1962 Constitution is that it is, in reality, substantially an import. It is not even so much a question that it ties Jamaica colonially to Britain; it is the fact that its legal concepts and constructs were not born out of the authentic Jamaican journey. The constitution might have been fashioned in a Kingston free-zone legal factory, but almost all of the components that went into its construction were imported from the United Kingdom. In the end, it still had to meet London's specifications. It might just as well have been

> Contentious questions about the structure of government that do not contribute significantly to economic advancement, a heightened sense of patriotic pride and national unity will not be worth the efforts they will require or the vexations they will spark.

---

[1]. Nettleford, Rex, Manley and the New Jamaica: 310

stamped "Made in England." Indeed, it remains "Orders in Council" and is still a grant from Her Majesty the Queen of England. Genuinely independent constitutions are usually agreements by the people of a nation and typically begin with, "We, the People . . ."

Prime Minister Portia Simpson Miller has telegraphed her intention to press for constitutional reforms that will result in the replacement of the queen as head of state. However, contentious questions about the structure of government that do not contribute significantly to economic advancement, a heightened sense of patriotic pride and national unity will not be worth the efforts they will require or the vexations they will spark. If, however, the attainment of a Jamaican republic will be tied to, and can result in, a greater sense of national identity and unity, then those efforts could represent a crucial launch pad and fillip for the construction of a better Jamaican society.

EQUALITY AND THE JUSTICE OF AFFIRMATIVE ACTION

Questions of social justice and a more egalitarian society have factored prominently in modern constitutional reform efforts in more developed societies, and particularly in those countries that are registering significant growth. In order to stimulate economic growth, most countries now recognize that they have to mainstream the economically marginalized masses that make up the base of their economies. This is a major deficiency in Jamaica's socioeconomic structure. In fact, Jamaica is increasingly moving in the opposite direction by extending the wealth gap and creating even more poor people.

The countries which are achieving growth have moved to correct the myopia of claims of growth without development or macroeconomic stability in runaway poverty. They have applied the full force of their respective constitutions to break the back of race, class, ethnic, and gender domination and exploitation. These countries have employed affirmative action policies in employment, education, and gender affairs. A few examples are cited below.

EMPLOYMENT EQUITY IN THE REPUBLIC OF SOUTH AFRICA

Affirmative action is enshrined in the South African Constitution. Section 9(2) provides that

> [e]quality includes the full and equal enjoyment of all rights and freedoms. To promote
> the achievement of equality, legislative and other measures designed to protect or advance
> persons, or categories of persons, disadvantaged by unfair discrimination may be taken.

The Employment Equity Act 1998 of the Republic of South Africa recognized that apartheid "created such pronounced disadvantages for certain categories of people that they cannot be redressed simply by repealing discriminatory laws." The act is designed "to redress the effects of discrimination." Section 6(1) prohibits employment discrimination on the basis of race, gender, sex, pregnancy, marital status, family responsibility, ethnic or social origin, colour, sexual orientation, age, disability, religion, HIV status, conscience, belief, political opinion, culture, language, and birth. Section 6(2) permits affirmative action discrimination for the attainment of employment equity.

The affirmative action policy is set out in Section 15. Section 15(c) requires employers to make "reasonable accommodation for people from designated groups in order to ensure that they enjoy equal opportunities and are equitably represented in the workforce of a designated employer." Section 1 is cogent and unrepentant. "Designated groups means black people, women, and people with disabilities." Designated employers are required to submit periodic reports to the director-general of the Labour Department, who is empowered through labour inspectors to monitor compliance and commence action in the Labour Court for breaches of the act.

EMPLOYMENT EQUITY IN CANADA

Canada's Constitutional Act 1982 includes a provision for affirmative action in its charter of rights and freedoms. Section 15 (2) reads,

> Subsection (1) does not preclude any law, program or activity that has as its object the amelioration of conditions of disadvantaged individuals or groups including those that are disadvantaged because of race, national or ethnic origin, colour, religion, sex, age, or mental or physical disability.

This provision recognizes that certain social groupings within the society have historically been disadvantaged by the prevailing social structures. The section has been given effect by the Canadian Employment Equity Act. The purpose of the act is set out in Section 2 as follows:

> The purpose of this Act is to achieve equality in the workplace so that no person shall be denied employment opportunities or benefits for reasons unrelated to ability and, in the fulfilment of that goal, to correct the conditions of disadvantage in employment experienced by women, aboriginal peoples, persons with disabilities and members of visible minorities by giving effect to the principle that employment equity means more than treating persons in the same way but also requires special measures and the accommodation of differences.

So for example, if a white male and an aboriginal female with similar qualifications applied for the same government job in Canada, by law, the aboriginal female should be employed ahead of the white male. The converse, of course, would have been certainly more likely in Jamaica, even in instances where the marginalized individual presented better employment credentials. Discrimination by colour, class, gender, and socioeconomic status is still prevalent in the Jamaican society.

GENDER EQUITY IN CHINA

The Constitution of the People's Republic of China has now constructed a complete legal system surrounding the rights and interests of women for the promotion of gender equality. These are spelt out in the Law on the Protection of the Rights and Interests of Women.[2] Article 11, for example, outlines that "[a]mong deputies to the National People's Congress and local people's congresses at various levels, there shall be an appropriate number of women deputies, the state will take measures, to gradually raise the proportion of women's deputies."

[2.] http://www.china-un.ch/eng/bjzl/t210715.htm

EDUCATION EQUITY IN BRAZIL

Article 5 of the Brazilian Constitution provides that, "All persons are equal before the law, *without any distinction whatsoever*" [author's emphasis]. This provision extends to everyone who is resident in Brazil, including foreigners. Despite this, the Federal Supreme Court has consistently upheld the constitutionality of reverse discrimination that applies quota preferences to Afro-Brazilian students. Essentially, Brazil has enforced race-related affirmative action in public educational institutions.[3]

EDUCATION EQUITY IN INDIA

Article 15(5): of the Constitution of India states that,

> "Nothing in this article or in sub-clause (*g*) of clause (1) of article 19 shall prevent the State from making any special provision, by law, for the advancement of any socially and educationally backward classes of citizens or for the Scheduled Castes or the Scheduled Tribes in so far as such special provisions relate to their admission to educational institutions *including private educational institutions, whether aided or unaided by the State* [author's emphasis], other than the minority educational institutions referred to in clause (1) of article 30."

AFFIRMATIVE ACTION IN JAMAICA

Affirmative action policies are now practiced in many countries, including the US, Israel, Sri Lanka, Japan, South Korea, Malaysia, New Zealand, and among several EU and Eastern European countries. Race, gender, and economic status as well as education, housing, employment, and social services considerations feature highly in the affirmative action policies of progressive nations. These issues must also impact any attempt to reform the Jamaican constitution.

Debt, corruption, criminality, and the absence of sustainable economic growth are directly related to Jamaica's inability to level the opportunity playing field and to correct its exaggerated, historical, colonial wealth distribution gaps. Development cannot be left to discretion and charity, and too many Jamaicans are still being kept in poverty on the fringes of society. The surest way to expand the economy is to mainstream the economically marginalized.

Affirmative action will be vigorously resisted by the principal beneficiaries of the current unjust national economic order and by those who wager on a better prospect under the current exploitative arrangement. Those who benefit from the current corrupt and unjust social and economic arrangement will buck, balk, and bully at even the slightest attempt to highlight the existing inequities. However, Jamaica cannot advance sufficiently without affirmative action in social and economic policies and programmes. In fact, the only logical conclusions to widespread injustice are an expansion of poverty and deprivation and an eventual catastrophic social upheaval.

[3.] Affirmative Action in Brazil: Reverse Discrimination and the Creation of Constitutionally Protected Color-line

It is the law and the government that must restrain exploitation and advance justice. All affirmative action or "positive discrimination" strategies really require for actualization is a government that is sufficiently committed to social justice and has the political will to push for equality of opportunities. In this information age, no opposition party that is serious about ever being elected to form the government would dare to publicly block moves to create greater economic balance for the people they propose to face in an election. Such a scandal could easily be construed and manipulated to follow its representatives into every polling booth in subsequent elections.

ELEMENTS OF AFFIRMATIVE ACTION

Public education, housing, and land management, for example, ought to be removed from the direct discretion of elected representatives and placed exclusively in trusts and managed with affirmative action guidelines. Education could be managed by a properly formalized and expanded National Education Trust, governing regional and local authorities. These trusts should be governed and funded after the pattern of the highly successful National Housing Trust. The Programme for the Advancement through Health and Education, PATH, should also be independently administered and aligned more closely to local government than central government. Considerations should also be given to the establishment of a National Employment Agency, with a central registry and accessible parish offices.

> The higher the number of Jamaicans that are kept landless, the higher the crime rate and the greater the risk of social disruption.

The thirty-sixth president of the United States of America, Lyndon B. Johnson, captured the essence of social justice with his observation that "we can only have a law abiding society if everyone has a stake in it." Dr. Basil Kong, a Jamaican-born psychologist, believes that "property ownership is the single most important ingredient for instilling respect for the law." He contends that "countries with wide distribution of land ownership tend to be more stable [and] prosperous," as land ownership is likely to discourage unruly behaviour and contains the prospect of improving respect for the rights of others. [4]

It follows logically then that the higher the number of Jamaicans that are kept landless, the higher the crime rate and the greater the risk of social disruption. A more enduring resolution to Jamaica's unusually high crime rate lies in comprehensive land reform and land distribution than in the much-preached increase in the number of police officers. Dr. Kong also argues that "by integrating 'extra-legals' into our legal system, we will release the aspirations and energies of poor people by giving them a stake in the country that they will want to protect."[5]

Order and peace are not identical. The order that emanates from peace is stable and enduring. Order without peace, on the other hand, is a social powder keg, and any spark can set it off. The single most prominent common denominator in progressive, contemporary constitutional reform efforts is that they strive conscientiously to achieve lasting peace by creating a better quality of life for excluded members of their respective populations. In the end, the penchant to suppress, as opposed to the tendency to liberate, is unquestionably a matter of one's socioeconomic vantage point. Justice begins at the point where powerbrokers are voluntarily, or involuntarily, made to see the perspectives

---

[4.] Kong, Basil Waine, "Creating Value of Dead Real Estate in Jamaica"
[5.] Ibid.

of the oppressed. Justice can be reformatory or revolutionary, but peace and prosperity begin when there is social consensus on justice.

BALANCED BOOK AND BALANCED LIVES

Prime Minister Portia Simpson Miller appears to be conscious of the prospects that affirmative action policies hold for national development. The prime minister has repeatedly articulated her grasp of "the importance of balancing the books, while balancing people's lives." Her own emphases on special provisions for affordable housing solutions for young professionals, the poor, and the disabled, and her stated intention for "Winner-City" development, as well as her government's support for targeted social investments in traditionally marginalized communities, underscore the government's grasp of the dynamics that govern the principles of reversed discrimination. She has also declared that

> "I say poverty reduction and its eventual elimination has to be a central plank of our policy, [if] growth and development is what we seek."
>
> —Portia Simpson Miller

> [w]hen I talk about the need to deal with poverty, when I emphasise the issue of poverty as one that must be dealt with decisively, there have been people who have sought to ridicule me. . . . But I say poverty reduction and its eventual elimination has to be a central plank of our policy, [if] growth and development is what we seek.[6]

The prime minister's heart appears to be in the right place. There is little doubt that she genuinely desires to do more to lift more of her people out of poverty. The same can be said of many of Jamaica's leaders through the years. No prime minister wants to fail or to be voted out of office. However, they have all been handicapped by the same limiting and constricting macroeconomic conditions that have resulted from the endemic and exploitative class divides, an ill-suited and inadequate legal system, and a combative political model that is completely inimical to Jamaica's progress.

The fundamental and far-reaching reforms, which are required to reverse the country's dismal economic performance over the years, cannot be attained within the current national political and economic structure. The massive electoral victory in 1989 was a rejection of trickle-down economics and probably a mandate for the resumption of the reform efforts of the 1970s. The landslide victory of 2011 was certainly a mandate to activate the promised "People Power." However, having suffered the overwhelming political defeat of 1980, the PNP has evidently become transformation-timid, preferring instead to stick with the changes that cannot be avoided and will not ruffle any powerful feathers. The JLP, which spearheaded the antitransformation movement between 1974 and 1980, has never demonstrated any serious inclination to upset the unjust class equation, which is at the root of all of Jamaica's political, legal, social, and economic challenges.

There can be no progress without transformation, and both political parties will have to do right by the people they purport to represent and work together to implement the required changes within a reasonable time frame. The disproportionate allocation of state resources, for example, is not currently backed by the force of law and could quite possibly be held to be proscribed in a court of law. Moreover, these critical and obligatory intervention programmes should not be left to the discretion

---

6.   In spite of Criticism, Portia says Still Committed to Poor, the *Gleaner*, July 24, 2013

or goodwill of respective administrations. Thomas Jefferson believed that "the care of human life and happiness, and not their destruction, is the first and only object of good government." He has also said, "Put not your faith in men, but bind them with the chains of the constitution."[7]

Affirmative action principles should be constitutionally authorized and supported by the enforcing legislative framework and administrative systems. These should be designed to enjoin successive governments and the relevant state agencies to the targeted advancement of historically marginalized groups and economically fringed communities within the society—and not just in a piecemeal manner. Systematic and legally sanctioned alienation of the broader mass of people has persisted for far too long, and the patchwork of incremental changes have simply prolonged the societal agony and intensified the deprivation among too many of the nation's people.

Growth and development are contiguous but not synonymous. In developing societies, uninformed political leaders who fail to grasp the distinctions between growth and development are often consigned to long periods on the opposition benches. Misguided administrations, which deceptively delineate "growth" from "development," often boast impressive book figures while social services are scaled back, education and training are neglected, and poverty increases. This economic myth should be finally and permanently debunked and rejected. Growth without appropriate levels of educational investment, for example, literally creates a fool's paradise. Growth without development is illusory, and succeeding generations will have to pick up the high price tag of the resulting underdevelopment. Macroeconomic stability without the requisite levels of social investment will have the same effect.

Philosophically and pragmatically, inequity and injustice—or corruption—cannot form sustainable bases for economic development. Governments that are serious about genuine and sustainable development give focus to equity and empowerment issues. Affirmative action cannot be dispensed in an incremental manner either. Affirmative incrementalism will result in a massive waste of resources, and the problems will persist, if not multiply (reference: Project Land Lease and Operation Pride, as examples). Affirmative action policies and programmes must be radical, comprehensive, and complete. However, governments that focus on the advancement of the economic base of their populations often register sustained medium- and long-term economic growth and realize remarkable economic development. They also tend to register impressive decreases in crime, violence, and corruption and create stable, progressive societies.

PARTICIPATION AND ACCOUNTABILITY IN GOVERNANCE

Democratization and participation in governance are not limited to the vote. Democracy is more properly pegged to opportunities for collective self-determination. The voice is the central concern of democracy. The vote is merely a consensus-facilitating mechanism. In the current constitutional framework, people participation in governance is very limited. Notwithstanding the mechanisms for the "vote of no confidence," essentially, there is no provision for the impeachment or recall of corrupt and ineffective elected officials until the completion of the term of office. Even so, because of the perpetuation of ignorance, political partisanship, and garrisons, there are still limits on electoral accountability.

[7.] The Kentucky Resolutions, 1798

The 1995 Final Report of the Joint Select Parliamentary Constitutional and Electoral Reform Committee recognized the public accountability loophole in the constitution and proposed impeachment mechanisms for serious misconduct "for all senior level public officials."[8] Successful impeachment would not preclude criminal liability. It is noteworthy that the committee felt that the issue was of sufficient importance to be included in the constitution. The committee also advanced proposals for the reform and entrenchment of the electoral process. Both concerns are closely related to an effective democratic process.

> The Jamaican constitution does not contain the possibility for expanded systems of accountability and has become a veritable roadblock to the progress of the nation.

As previously noted, parliamentary democracy is established on the maintenance of classism within the social structure. It resists all attempts to hold the ruling classes accountable. This is quite clearly evidenced in the fact that the Jamaican "elected aristocracy" has stalled constitutional reforms, local government reforms, justice reforms, impeachment provisions, and the attempts to institute a special prosecutor. Consciously or unconsciously, every attempt to bring about more accountability of public officials and greater participation by the people in governance have been blocked, hijacked, and railroaded.

The Jamaican constitution does not contain the possibility for expanded systems of accountability and has become a veritable roadblock to the progress of the nation. In effect, it has ganged up with those who resent and resist the democratization of governance and progress for the broad mass of the people. It is little surprise, therefore, that the Jamaican society and economy remains in such a pathetic shape. It is not likely to improve under the current governance framework. In fact, there is the distinct likelihood that it will get worse because the constitution does not hold leaders to account and does not provide adequate protection for the people from administrative and class abuse. Indeed, it leaves them vulnerable to social alienation and economic exploitation.

TABLE 5: PROPOSED CONSTITUTIONAL CHANGES

RECOMMENDED CONSTITUTIONAL CHANGES
Simplify the language of the constitution
Make the constitution accessible to the people
Establish affirmative action policies for employment
Establish affirmative action policies in education, land ownership, and housing
Entrench affirmative action policies for economically marginalized persons and communities

---

8. Final Report of the Joint Select Committee of the Houses of Parliament on Constitutional and Electoral Reform: 20

CHAPTER SEVEN

REFORMATION AND THE ECONOMY

Economic development is effected at two basic levels: the preparation of the economy for growth and the actual growing of the economy. Both are complementary. The constitution can facilitate growth by creating the context and "rolling the wicket" for growth. The target areas are

1. education, training, and resocialization for growth;
2. improved labour relations and workforce productivity;
3. removing the impediments and obstacles to growth; and
4. controlling and constraining the elements that militate against growth.

No economy can grow unless the population generally possesses the requisite productivity and educational skills and the appetite and aptitude for growth. The constitution can be formulated to facilitate these elements. The constitution can also provide the basis for the machinations that reduce the waste of resources occasioned by the high cost of security, remediation, corruption, pollution, and environmental degradation. Most of the solutions to these types of drain on the economy are rooted in education and economic justice.

The constitution can also lay the basis, through affirmative action, to ensure that more women and other marginalized groups are equipped for, and brought into, productivity. This is particularly important since women typically work harder and contribute more to the care of their families and economic disruptions often emanate from disgruntled and excluded social groups. At the baseline, the constitution should be designed to unlock the innovative and creative instinct of the extraordinary and longsuffering Jamaican people.

REFORMATION, ECONOMIC DEVELOPMENT, AND PROSPERITY

The People's Republic of China has maintained the fastest-growing economy in the world for at least a decade. China continues to record impressive growth, and it did so even within the context of the worst global economic recession for a lifetime. China's record growth has not just resulted from their population size or the renowned enterprise and frugality of the Chinese people. Their impressive economic growth has emanated from a deliberate policy framework for growth and is principally a creature of their comprehensive constitutional reform efforts, which began in earnest in 1982.

Below is a summary of the economic growth initiatives that have been activated by the Chinese constitution. The full text is contained in appendix 4.

Article 14 of the Chinese constitution specifically mandates that the state is to continuously raise labour productivity and improve economic results "by enhancing the enthusiasm of the working people." This is to be achieved through raising the levels of the technical skill of workers, and by "disseminating advanced science and technology, improving the systems of economic administration and enterprise operation and management, instituting the socialist system of responsibility in various forms and improving organization of work." The state is also required to practice strict economy, combat waste, manage consumption and balance "the interests of the collective and the individual as well as of the State and, gradually, improve the material and cultural life of the people."

Article 15 authorizes the state to practice economic planning and ensure "the proportionate and coordinated growth of the national economy through overall balancing by economic planning and the supplementary role of regulation by the market." It also holds that "disturbance of the orderly functioning of the social economy or disruption of the state economic plan by any organization or individual is prohibited."

Article 16 gives state enterprises "decision-making power in operation and management within the limits prescribed by law." State enterprises are required to "fulfil all their obligations under the state plan" and practice "democratic management through congresses of workers and staff and in other ways in accordance with the law."

Article 17 grants decision-making power to collective economic organizations in the conduct of independent economic activities, on condition that they accept the guidance of the state plan and abide by the relevant laws and practice "democratic management in accordance with the law, with the entire body of their workers electing or removing their managerial personnel and deciding on major issues concerning operation and management."

Article 18 focuses the state on "foreign enterprises." All foreign enterprises and other foreign economic organizations in China, as well as joint ventures with Chinese and foreign investment located in China, are required to "abide by the law of the People's Republic of China." However, the lawful rights and interests of foreign investors "are protected by the law of the People's Republic of China."

PRACTICAL ECONOMIC LESSONS FROM CHINA

Basically, the Chinese economic successes have resulted from a comprehensive and systematic process that has been enshrined in their constitution. That is how important economic development is to the Chinese state. The phenomenal growth of the national economy of the People's Republic of China has essentially been established on four critical economic pillars:

1. The raising of the enthusiasm and productivity of the nation's workers
2. Coordinated and proportionate economic planning by the state and the limitation of economic disturbance and economic waste
3. Democratic decision making at the workplace, which most surely expands the idea pool and enhances the sense of "ownership"
4. Deliberate and determined pursuit of foreign direct investments

All of these elements can be easily and successfully adapted and implemented in both public and private sector economic enterprises in Jamaica. However, it must also be carefully noted that the Chinese Republic employed state intervention in economic enterprises and felt that economic development was of such a critical concern that it required constitutional authority. In addition, the Jamaican business community requires an enhanced sense of patriotic pride, improved social commitment, and better entrepreneurial and technological capabilities. It also needs to pursue practical strategies to raise the enthusiasm, loyalty, and productivity of their employees.

However China's growth is assessed or construed, what is undeniable is that China has grown economically and continues to register significant growth and this means that their growth strategy has worked effectively. There has been much talk about growth in Jamaica over many decades. The country can either choose to continue the empty chatter and wishful thinking or seek actively to replicate the strategies that can be adapted successfully. In the end, the Chinese economic formula appears to point the Jamaican government to the need to

1. prioritize economic growth and reflect this in the national budget;
2. craft a long-term macroeconomic plan and ground it in the constitution;
3. contain crime and corruption and remedy economic waste;
4. amplify the energy, enthusiasm, and productivity of Jamaican workers and industries;
5. democratize the Jamaican workplace and expand employment justice to create more scope for better wages and working conditions and a greater influx of ideas; and
6. move even more aggressively to attract foreign direct investments, as well as to
7. expand Jamaican enterprises in other countries, starting perhaps with the Jamaican Diaspora, the Spanish-speaking Caribbean states, and Central and South America.

STATE-SPONSORED EMPLOYEE SHAREHOLDER COMPANIES

Within the Jamaican context, state participation in business activities can be facilitated through the divestment of business-viable state enterprises into tightly regulated employee shareholder companies. Although the government would continue to be a major client of these new companies, it is not inconceivable that their client base could be expanded over time to include even offshore engagements. At the very least, the government would quite easily achieve, along with an administrative divestment of local government, a dramatic reduction in the number of public servants. Over the medium to long term, this managed reduction of the public sector would obviously have a positive impact on the government's wage bill and pension payments. This approach represents a more progressive way to deal with the disproportionate public wage bill and pension payments than simply to axe public servants or reduce social services.

DEBT MANAGEMENT AND NATIONAL DEVELOPMENT

Section 120(1) of the Jamaican Constitution mandates that public debt is charged on the Consolidated Fund and augments the priority of loan repayment. Thomas Jefferson has been reported to have said that, "I place economy among the first and most important virtues, and public debt as the greatest of dangers. To preserve our independence, we must not let our rulers load us with perpetual debt," and further that, "the principle of spending money to be paid by future generations, under the name of funding, is but swindling futurity on a large scale." "Swindling" is a very strong word and a serious rebuke but when one seriously contemplates the heavy toll the public debt burden has taken on Jamaica's human development, Jefferson's conclusion is irrefutable. Jamaica's leaders, past, present and future should take careful note.

> "The principle of spending money to be paid by future generations, under the name of funding, is but swindling futurity on a large scale."
>
> —*Thomas Jefferson*

The current government has already recognized the need to constrain and contain government borrowing and has moved, through legislation, to hold successive governments to a tighter regulatory regime for public borrowing. However, many well-intentioned laws have been passed by parliament that have had limited effects on the manner in which the country is governed or how the economy is managed. Debt management is one of Jamaica's most pressing economic challenges, and it is critical to national development. In the spirit of this discussion, it is clear that debt management is also a constitutional issue.

ECONOMIC JUSTICE

Employment injustice that results in poor productivity, economic stagnation which limits national development, and the overwhelming debt burden are three of Jamaica's most significant and enduring challenges. They have given rise to many of the country's social ills, and the constricted, nearly nonexistent fiscal space they create is at the root of the government's inability to successfully address all other national problems, including crime, justice, educational development, infrastructural improvement, and social services delivery. Economic development is consequently Jamaica's number one priority. In the final analysis, as Bill Clinton—who presided over, arguably, one of the most economically successful periods in recent US history—has said, "It's the economy, stupid."

LABOUR RELATIONS AND PRODUCTIVITY

Another potentially contentious element in the economic life of Jamaica is labour relations. Even though Jamaica has boasted progressive labour laws since the comprehensive reviews, which were conducted between 1972 and 1976, serious gaps still exists between the spirit of the laws and the practice at the Jamaican workplace. This dissonance raises questions about the articulation and enforcement of the labour laws. Clearly, after forty years with virtually no change, these laws are also long overdue for a comprehensive overhaul.

It could also be successfully argued that whereas the current labour laws provided some well-needed relief to workers at the time of formulation, they have not been as effective in the transformation of the labour landscape. Arguing from different sides of the political divide, senators and union leaders Lambert Brown and Kavan Gayle found common cause in their emphatic calls, on separate motions, for a review of elements of the country's labour laws.[1] While this underscores the need for a revision of the laws, it is felt here that legislation alone is not sufficient to finally remove, what

---

[1.] Motions debated in the Senate on October 26, 2012

the late Dudley Thompson once referred to as, "the smell of Slavery"[2] from the Jamaican labour landscape. An "economic constitution" must employ the power of the law to force a dramatic attitudinal change in the local workplace because, especially as it pertains to wages, the scent of slavery still persists in too many Jamaican workplaces.

There are those who rush to the conclusion that the general lack of productivity in the Jamaican workplace is significantly related to the diminished output by the Jamaican worker. These individuals are often quick to call for a balance between the rights of the workers and the rights of the employers. However, even a casual reference to the fact that Jamaica has one of the most oppressive wealth distribution records and one of the most scandalous income disparity gaps in the entire western hemisphere will indicate where that "balance" is in fact to be placed. It is therefore completely deceitful and utterly disgraceful that any representative of the people should even begin to tout a "balance" that would require Jamaican workers to surrender more.

The labour myth that has been perpetuated for generations by elements within the Jamaican society, which claims that the average Jamaica worker is inherently lazy and a habitual pilferer, needs to be "finally and permanently discredited and abandoned." Are these not the same Jamaicans who excel at any task as employees in other countries and the same Jamaicans who are credited by tourists as being among the friendliest and most hospitable hotel workers in the world? Are these not the same Jamaicans labourers who are likely to harass their own relatives over the property of bosses who treat them well? Are these not the same Jamaicans who work two or three jobs at a time in places where they receive reasonable wages for their labour? And are these not the same Jamaicans who are among the most-sought-after workers for the heavy lifting on US and Canadian farms and in their hotel rooms and the delicate touch in their schools and hospitals?

It seems fairly obvious, therefore, that there are other productivity variables at play within the Jamaican workplace. Consequently, this discussion is predicated on the assertions that

1. there is greater corruption, waste, extravagance, and laziness, at infinitely much greater costs to the economy, higher up on the food chain than among regular Jamaican workers.
2. Jamaican workers possesses an inordinately high capacity for loyalty to employers who treat them with respect and accord them the appropriate dignity as fellow human beings and essential partners in business.
3. given just wages and favourable working conditions, the Jamaican worker is unquestionably one of the most enterprising, productive, and cooperative employee in the world.
4. the fact is many Jamaican labourers and craftsmen possess a pride in their work that borders on obsessive compulsive disorder. There are many domestic helpers and gardeners, for example, who will clean the daylight into their employers' houses and yards.

> The extent to which Jamaica will record economic growth is therefore integrally related to the manner in which Jamaican workers are treated.

Given these premises and based on the evidence of the almost unparalleled successes of migrant Jamaican workers and the vast majority of Jamaicans abroad, it becomes apparent that the persistent exploitation of Jamaican workers at home and their resulting passive rebellion of diminished productivity is a significant impediment to

---

2. Dudley Thompson, Senate Debate on "The Act to Repeal the Master and Servant Law," May 31, 1974

the economic progress of the nation. The extent to which Jamaica will record economic growth is therefore integrally related to the manner in which Jamaican workers are treated. They do not even ask for respect or decent working conditions. All they require is fair wages. The truth is many of those who deride the regular Jamaican worker would perhaps not be able to survive beyond one of the measly paychecks they give them.

CONSTITUTIONAL REFORM AND LABOUR RELATIONS

The word "worker" does not appear in the Jamaican constitution at all. Again, this omission is related to the colonial mind-set that accompanied the crafting of the constitution. To understand how significant an oversight this is, one has to contrast this lapse, for example, with the constitutions of Cuba and China. The entire Cuban constitution appears to have been formulated on the centrality and worth of the Cuban worker. Article 1 reads as follows:

> Cuba is an independent and sovereign socialist state of workers, organized with all and for the good of all as a united and democratic republic, for the enjoyment of political freedom, social justice, individual and collective well-being and human solidarity.

Enshrined in the preamble of the constitution of the People's Republic of China is the declaration that "[i]n building socialism it is imperative to rely on the workers, peasants and intellectuals and unite with all the forces that can be united." Here, workers are accorded a position of preeminence as the first of the three named groups that comprise the Chinese society. This is augmented by Article 1, which emphasizes that "the People's Republic of China is a socialist state under the people's democratic dictatorship led by the working class and based on the alliance of workers and peasants."

In recognition of the importance of the worker to national development and in contemplation of employment justice, the Federative Republic of Brazil has entrenched labour laws in Article 7 of its constitution (see the full chapter in appendix 3). Among the more progressive considerations [with author's emphases] are

- *unemployment insurance*, in the event of involuntary unemployment;
- guarantee of wages never below the minimum one, for those receiving variable pay;
- *year-end one-salary bonus* based on the full pay or on the amount of the pension;
- wage protection, as provided by law, with felonious withholding of wages being a crime;
- *participation in the profits* or results, independent of wages, and, exceptionally, participation in the management of the company, defined by law;
- *family allowance* for their dependents;
- annual vacation with remuneration at least one third higher than the normal salary;
- *paternity leave*, under the terms established by law;
- retirement pension;
- *protection of the labour market for women* through specific incentives, as provided by law;
- additional remuneration for strenuous, unhealthy or dangerous work, as established by law;
- *free assistance for children and dependents* from birth to six years of age, in day-care centres and preschool facilities;
- prohibition of any discrimination with respect to wages and hiring criteria of handicapped workers;

- *prohibition of any distinction between manual, technical and intellectual work* or among the respective professionals; and
- equal rights for workers with a permanent employment bond and for sporadic workers.

Interestingly, Article 8 also "prohibits the dismissal of a unionized employee from the moment of the registration of his candidacy to a position of union direction or representation and, if elected, even if as a substitute, up to one year after the end of his term in office, unless he commits a serious fault as established by law."

It is difficult to determine the extent to which these labour laws have contributed to the rapid expansion of the Brazilian economy. What is certain is that given these laws, average Brazilian workers are likely to be more enthusiastic about the profitability of the company to which they are employed. It can surely be contended that labour laws bear close relation to productivity. In light of the comprehensive protection and the humanizing effect that these laws provide for the Brazilian worker, and given the fact that they are ensconced in their constitution, one is led to think that the Jamaican workers' unions and the Jamaican legislators have been sleeping on the job for the past forty years. It is little wonder then that Jamaica continues to register such poor growth figures.

> Sustainable economic growth *cannot* be achieved without economic justice. Therefore, the fight for reasonable wages in any sector is a fight for the economic advancement of the entire nation.

How Jamaica could have moved from some of the most progressive labour laws in the world in the 1970s to some of the most exploitative labour conditions today defies logic. What is even more astonishing is how mute the memoranda-muzzled trade unions and workers' organizations—such as the Jamaica Teachers Association, the Jamaica Civil Service Association and the Nurses Association of Jamaica—have become. Their absenteeism has contributed significantly to the economic decline of the country as they have been standing silently by as more and more wealth is being extracted, by the billions, by the voracious minority from the straitened majority they purport to represent.

Reduced income disparity is one of the most critical factors for economic development in any country, and if Jamaica's economy is to recover and grow, the workers must reclaim the justice of appropriate wages. Wage freezes, restrictions, and "restraints," which only target the poor and middle class, are certain prescriptions for economic exploitation and wealth transfer. Sustainable economic growth *cannot* be achieved without economic justice. Therefore the fight for reasonable wages in any sector is a fight for the economic advancement of the entire nation. The unions must stop selling out the people's livelihood and begin to do their jobs proficiently.

Modern Jamaica was established through the labour struggles of the 1930s on effective workers' representation. The fight for workers' rights is part of the very DNA of the nation, and the economy cannot grow or prosper without vigilant workers' representation. The country is dying because the unions have gone into prolonged representational hibernation. Instead, they have been busy keeping the country "stable" for the big bosses so that the debt can be paid, while wealth continues to be transferred at a mind-blowing rate and the workers starve. Unions are expected to carry on the tradition of the freedom fighters. They should always fight on the side of the people. Had the unions been effective, Jamaica could not have ended up with possibly the worst income disparity in the entire western hemisphere. The unions must acknowledge that they have failed their people miserably, do their penance, and "wheel and come again."

INDUSTRIAL COURT

The current labour dispute mechanisms often require the intervention of the minister of Labour to settle disputes related to wage and working conditions. Barbados successfully deals with labour disputes, and in a far less contentious manner, through the Industrial Court. Serious thought should be given to the formalization of the Industrial Disputes Tribunal into an Industrial Court, and since productivity is of such importance to Jamaica's survival, this court should also have constitutional status. Concessions would of course have to be constitutionally created to permit union and personal representation before such an Industrial Court.

TABLE 6: PROPOSED CONSTITUTIONAL FRAMEWORK

RECOMMENDED CONSTITUTIONAL FRAMEWORK	
Chapter I	– Preliminary
Chapter II	– Citizenship: Definition and Citizens' Charter
Chapter III	– Charter of Fundamental Rights and Freedoms, *with Affirmative Action provisions for Land Ownership, Housing, Education, Social Security, Welfare, Gender Parity and the Disabled*
Chapter IV	– PILLAR A – The Legislature, *with considerations about Minority/Majority Leaders, reviews of the Senate, the Senate President, House Speaker, and Parliamentary Committees*
Chapter V	– PILLAR B – The Executive, *with a Republican Model of Government with Partial Separation of Powers and a popularly elected Prime Minister*
Chapter VI	– PILLAR C – The Judicature, *with or without the CCJ, but with expanded Community and Regional Dispute Resolution Systems*
Chapter VII	– PILLAR D – Public Accountability, *including Impeachment and Recall*
Chapter VIII	– The Administration of Justice, *incorporating a truly independent Attorney General, Justice Reform and Independent Funding for the Judiciary*
Chapter IX	– National Security, *with social justice considerations*
Chapter X	– Financial Management, *including Taxation, Tax Collection, and Debt Management*
Chapter XI	– The Economy, *with planned Productivity, Growth, and Development Strategies*
Chapter XII	– Labour Relations, *including Employment Justice and an Industrial Court*
Chapter XIII	– The Public Service, *including Efficiency and Accountability*
Chapter XIV	– Constitutional Offices, *including the Office of the Special Prosecutor*
Chapter XV	– Local Government, *with Autonomy, Entrenchment, and Independent Revenue Systems*
Chapter XVI	– The Electoral Process
Chapter XVII	– Miscellaneous

REFORMATION AND ACCOUNTABILITY

One of the major challenges with the constitution and the development of Jamaica is that there is a distinct disconnect between the constitution as the primary legal infrastructure and the government and the people of Jamaica. The provisions of the constitution are not promoted by the government and are not generally known by the people. Notwithstanding the inherent flaws and deficiencies in the constitution, if, for example, the fundamental rights contained therein were zealously promulgated by the administration and widely known by the population, those rights could possibly have contributed to more social cohesion, less exploitation, and a greater respect for life and human rights by state agencies and regular citizens.

THE CABINET, THE PARLIAMENT AND THE CONSTITUTION

The constitution must be reconstituted to establish broad social and economic development ideals and regain preeminence as the legal touchstone of the country. The gap must be bridged between the objectives of the constitution and the purposes and policies of government. It is the constitution that must inform the legislative agenda and drive the administrative processes and the administration of justice. In order to achieve this, the parliament, the executive, and all branches of the administration must be reconfigured in service of the constitution. In such an arrangement, each cabinet member ought to be governed by, and required to give effect to, and account to a relevant parliamentary committee for specific sections of the constitution. Table 7 below advances a template on which this system could be formulated.

TABLE 7: PROPOSED EXECUTIVE CONFIGURATION

CABINET PORTFOLIO	PARLIAMENTARY COMMITTEE	CONSTITUTIONAL RESPONSIBILITY
1. Foreign Affairs, Foreign Trade, and Diaspora Affairs	1. Foreign Relations	– Nationhood and Definition of State, Foreign Relations, Foreign Trade, and the Diaspora
2. Citizenship and Human Rights (MP)	2. Citizenship, Human Rights, and Social Services	– Citizenship: Definition and Charter
3. Land and Environment 4. Housing and Water 5. Human Resource Development (*Education and Training*) 6. Health and Social Security		– Charter of Fundamental Rights and Freedoms, with affirmative action provisions for Land Ownership, Housing, Education and Training, Health, Social Security, Welfare, Gender Affairs, and the Disabled
7. Legislative Affairs	3. House Committee	– PILLAR A – The Legislature
8. Prime Minister	4. Executive Powers	– PILLAR B – The Executive

9. Justice	5. Justice and Public Accountability	– PILLAR C – The Judicature
		– PILLAR D – Public Accountability
		– The Administration of Justice
		– Constitutional Offices related to Justice
10. Public Service, Commerce, and Trade (MP)	6. Public Service	– The Public Service
		– Constitutional Offices related to Public Service
11. Finance and Planning (MP)	7. Public Accounts	– Financial Management
12. National Security (MP)	8. National Security	– National Security
13. Economic Development and Industry (MP) 14. Agriculture 15. Tourism and Culture 16. Science, Energy, and Technology 17. Infrastructure and Transport	9. Economic Development, Industry, and Production	– The Economy, with growth strategies, such as 1. Agricultural Self-Sufficiency and Agro-Processing 2. Tourism and Cultural Industry Expansion 3. Science and Technology-based Economy and Energy efficiency 4. Modern Infrastructure Development
18. Employment	10. Employment	– Labour Relations and workforce productivity
19. Community Development, Youth, and Sports	11. Local Government, Community Development, and Parish Council oversight	– Local Government
20. Cabinet Secretary (*Information*)	12. Electoral Affairs	– Electoral Affairs

The transformation of the culture and structure of the legislature is critical to Jamaica's development. Apart from a reduction in the number of MPs and their reorientation from welfare officers to state legislators, there is also the need for a reorganization of the committees of parliament to enable the legislature to effectively advance the aims and intentions of the constitution and fulfil its watchdog role. Clearly, committee chairmen would have to be remunerated and resourced in a manner that would enable them to efficiently manage their respective committees. This raises issues of dedicated funding for the legislature. It would also be important for the committees to understand that in addition to the checks and balances they are to provide for the executive, they would also be an integral part of the search for solutions to national challenges.

The republican prime minister would also be required to report to parliament. This could be facilitated by an annual state of nation report—replacing the Throne Speech—to the people's representatives in parliament and the constitutional watchdogs in the senate before each budget is presented for approval. This could be followed by a budget presentation by the finance minister in parliament, and a state of the nation debate in both houses, which would be designed to tackle the deficiencies and defaults in the government's social and economic stewardship and human rights record. These could replace the often-contentious grandstanding of the budget debate and the laborious sectoral presentations. The sectoral presentations should be made—with provisions for questions, answers, critique, and recommendations—to the respective parliamentary oversight committees. These sectoral presentations ought to be given by each cabinet member in the form of annual reports for the preceding year and programme outlines for the succeeding year—as a CEO would present a report to a board of directors.

A new multichamber parliament building should facilitate the concurrent taking of multiple presentations to expedite the business of the nation. The parliament is the nerve center of a progressive nation and is typically a microcosm of the general health of the country. It should present absolutely no surprise that a country with a legislature that has had to borrow its parliament building for more than half a century would also have such a colossal debt burden. Any state that cannot find the resources or the leadership for a proper parliament building after more fifty years of independence is not likely to be a progressing nation and might have been better off remaining a colony. A legislature that cannot build itself a house is surely going to struggle to make its nation prosperous. Talk is excessive and announcements are numerous, but the pace of progress in Jamaica, on even basic elements like a parliament building, is excruciatingly unhurried. This must change quickly.

CHAPTER EIGHT

THE HOPE OF REFORMATION

TRANSFORMATION VERSUS INCREMENTALISM

Historically, traditionalists and the principal beneficiaries of unjust economic systems often make out convincing arguments for gradual or incremental change. These persons favour the passing of a plethora of "Band-Aid laws," often inundating, and overwhelming the Office of the Parliamentary Counsel, as they scamper frantically to assuage the mounting impatience of the people and to stem the social and economic hemorrhages that threaten their oppressive comfort zones. What they are really doing is to slow down social justice and defend their bourgeoisie privileges at the expense of the progress of the nation.

> Almost without exception, the countries that are posting impressive economic growth have conducted far-reaching economic and justice-related revisions of their constitutions.

On the other side of the debate, however, are equally cogent positions that are often not systematically argued, primarily because radicalism has been rendered outmoded and radicals are often kept in check by their more powerful, influential and conservative, autocratic, and neocolonial political overlords. Among the reasons why reformation is preferred to incrementalism within the context of this discourse are the following:

1. The philosophical base of the existing Jamaican constitution was formulated in a completely different context with an entirely different set of aspirations and objectives from what Jamaica requires today. The political constitution of 1962 helped to attain self-government. Jamaica now needs a social and economic constitution to comprehensively address the current and future needs of its people.
2. It is virtually impossible to construct a republican form of government and realize genuine people power from a parliamentary democracy which fundamentally does not support active, ongoing people participation in governance.
3. The constitution is an integrated legal document with many continuous threads and areas of overlap. The pulling of any single loose thread could result in the unraveling of other aspects of the constitution. (Reference, for example, the Privy Council decision in the CCJ case or the attempts to establish a special prosecutor.)
4. Judging from the pace at which legislation moves through the Jamaican parliament and the extensive nature of the reviews that are required, a gradual or incrementalist approach to constitutional transformation would take decades to achieve. This would be further

exacerbated by the distractions that will be created by the myriad of pressing social and economic challenges with which the society grapples and the traditional political posturing and partisanship by the elected aristocracy and their shadow puppet masters.

5. Incremental changes are likely to have the same effect as the grant of independence. They will not go far enough in achieving the fundamental changes that the Jamaican society urgently needs. They will simply create a pacifier effect as they seek to keep dissatisfied and discontented citizens under subjugation.

6. Continuous revisions of the constitution are likely to adversely impact the sacrosanct nature of the constitution and erode the "predictability and certainty of law." A complete modern constitution should be formulated and put to the people for ratification.

7. Most importantly, the Jamaican economy is hovering on the brink and it is in too sickly a state for first aid remedies. It is in dire need of the comprehensive corrective surgery that only constitutional reform can achieve. Jamaica's legal system does not need a paramedic; it needs a surgeon.

The most practical and compelling reason, however, for a comprehensive constitutional transformation is the fact that almost without exception, the countries that are posting impressive economic growth or realizing reasonable economic stability have conducted far-reaching economic and social justice-related revisions of their constitutions. It was incrementalism that brought Jamaica to its current economic conundrum and incrementalism is not likely to be the means of resolution.

REFERENDUM

A referendum is not an absolute necessity if broad political consensus can be achieved. However, extensive constitutional changes that are backed by the expressed democratic support of the general population can significantly improve the effectiveness of the constitution. This is also likely to embolden state agencies to fast-track and effect required changes. A referendum can also provide the additional benefit of forcing all sectors of the population to pay careful attention to the constitutional provisions that are being enacted on their behalf. Incrementalism, such as the Charter of Rights, can easily slip by without the knowledge of the primary target beneficiaries.

Garfield Higgins believes that "the PNP has suffered with referendum-phobia" since 1961. However, if properly managed—beginning with a general consensus among all the country's political factions and with extensive national consultations, education, and marketing—a referendum that focuses the hopes and the aspirations of the greater mass of the Jamaican population *cannot* fail.

The arguments that a referendum is too costly or that the Jamaica population cannot handle multiple issues on a single ballot, say for example if a referendum is twinned with a general election to reduce costs, are simply not true. The average Jamaican can easily distinguish complex political issues. For those who think a referendum is too expensive, they need to look at the alternative: decades of more economic stagnation and the constant threat of social upheaval. This same "interventionalist" argument was applied to the remedial financial sector bailout of the mid-1990s, and look at the debt burden and economic frustrations it has spawned. It is always better to pay the cost price upfront than to pay later with the accumulated compound interests after the crisis.

The current political leaders have to emulate their forerunners and trust the people, even where the results do not advance their personal political and economic prospects. Our leaders must endeavour to activate the hard-won independence legacy of self-determination and give the people their voice. The vote alone has not served their social and economic causes well.

THE COST OF THE CONSTITUTION

Peter Phillips, Audley Shaw, Omar Davies, and Edward Seaga, four of Jamaica's five most recent ministers of finance, have all questioned or lamented the sluggish pace of economic growth. The conclusion here is that they have all been given a straw basket of a flawed socioeconomic legal framework to carry economic growth and development. Consequently, economic growth and the promise of prosperity have and will continue to leak away until a government is bold enough to tackle the fundamental constitutional and social transformation that will change Jamaica's historically dismal growth trajectory.

Except for Michael Manley's recognition that administrative tinkering was irresponsible, every post-independent cabinet has failed to understand that a prosperous country cannot be built on rampant inequality and all have failed to implement the requisite changes to cauterize the social and economic hemorrhages. Edward Seaga, for example, as minister of finance and planning, raised the issue of tax avoidance on Ministry Paper No. 18 over forty-five years ago on May 8, 1969, and until now, what he termed then as "the evasion of tax by unlawful means and avoidance of tax by finding legal loopholes" have never been sufficiently plugged. In fact, it might be worse today than in 1969 because Mr. Shaw, his immediate JLP successor as finance minister, said in 2009 that he estimated that there were at least 200,000 Jamaicans—who presumably should be—were not paying any income tax.[1]

No financial wizard, however accomplished and determined, can achieve sustainable development with these levels of tax dodging, such obvious and pervasive economic oppression of the broader mass of the population, such a large multitude of perpetually poverty-stricken people, and such a myriad of social challenges. The fundamentals of Jamaica's socioeconomic arrangements are inherently wrong. Nearly every economically advancing country on the globe has at some stage of their history come to this conclusion and made the required constitutional adjustments. Jamaica must also find the leadership with the courage to follow suit or be condemned to a never-ending cycle of bullet-biting austerity measures and the associated bitter medicine of fixing economic stagnation and contraction. Administrative tinkering is still irresponsible, if not blatantly dishonest.

The cost of the current constitution and the social and economic injustices it has undergirded, fashioned, and entrenched over the past thirty years is incalculable. The cost of the consistently high rates of crime and violence, for example, has been conservatively estimated at 7.1 percent of GDP annually. If this is measured over the forty years of its existence since the mid-1970s, it tells a gruesome tale of the slaughter of human life and potential and a heartbreaking history of economic destruction. Hundreds of billions of dollars of public funds are squandered and transferred to private pockets each year. When corruption, tax dodging, low productivity, high-interest debt repayment, various types of social dysfunctions and disruptions, the cost of security, the price tag of all forms of remediation, and all the other types of economic sinkholes are totaled, then it has been nothing

---

1.   Jamaica Information Service, Shaw Warns Against Tax Evasion, April 4, 2009

short of a miracle that Jamaica has been able to post any growth at all. It is an even greater wonder that the society has remained relatively stable. Indeed, Jamaicans are a patient and long-suffering people.

The methodology has been questioned, but no one can really fault the government for moving with such "fixity of purpose" to ease the crushing debt burden off the backs of the Jamaican poor and middle class. The debt is the most obvious economic challenge, and the intentions are unquestionably noble. However, the debt is a mere symptom of the enduring economic malady. The debt is like the joint pain of CHIKV, and fixing it is but a dose of pain medicine. It might temporarily ease the misery, but it will not eliminate the inflammation, and the suffering will return with a vengeance. The government must also find and eradicate all the wealth-sucking, disease-spreading parasites in the economy through a complete clean-up of the legal system. It must identify the deeply embedded breeding grounds and apply a comprehensive constitutional vector control to exterminate the virus so that there will be no economic relapse and future generations will not be similarly afflicted.

> The debt is like the joint pain of CHIKV, and fixing it is but a dose of pain medicine. It might temporarily ease the misery, but it will not eliminate the inflammation, and the suffering will return.

TABLE 8: THE COST OF JAMAICA'S UNJUST SOCIAL AND ECONOMIC LEGAL CONFIGURATION

SOCIAL FACTOR	ECONOMIC COST
High Crime and Violence and the High Cost of Security	"Ward et al. (2009) estimated that the direct medical cost of injuries due to interpersonal violence accounted for nearly 12% of Jamaica's total health expenditure in 2006, while productivity losses due to interpersonal violence-related injuries accounted for approximately 4% of Jamaica's GDP. If the latter is added to the estimate of security costs by Francis et al., then the combined total is 7.1% of Jamaica's GDP."[2] The annualized cost of 7.1% of Jamaica's GDP is over $100 billion.
High Levels of Tax Dodging	In 2012, of the over 62,000 companies purportedly operating in Jamaica, only about 17,000 (28%) registered for tax purposes. From this, only about 6,000 (10%) filed tax returns and only about 3,000 (5%) paid any taxes at all.[4] Property tax compliance fell by approximately 25% between 2003 and 2010, contributing to a decline from 0.25% to 0.10% of GDP.[5] In 2009, Audley Shaw said, "It is estimated that there are at least 200,000 Jamaicans who are not paying any income tax today."[6]

---

[2]   Professor Anthony Clayton of the University of the West Indies, in a report prepared for the Ministry of National Security, entitled A New Approach: National Security Policy for Jamaica, quoted by James, Ewin, in The Economic Cost of Crime, The Jamaica Observer, Saturday, March 02, 2013

[3]   Programme of Advancement through Health and Education, PATH and Jamaica Emergency Employment Programme, JEEP

High Cost of Welfare and Social Intervention	Billions of dollars are pumped yearly, from public and private sources, into welfare, poverty alleviation, and remediation efforts, such as the PATH and JEEP programmes and the charitable efforts of the diaspora.[3]
High Levels of Corruption	Fixing a price to corruption over the years since the first major public scandal of the school building project of the 1960s would likely make even the most grounded dizzy.
Greed, Economic Exploitation, High Debt, and High Interest Rates	Jamaica has the highest debt interest rate in the world. Interest payment on the public debt has gobbled up the lion's share of the budget for many years. In 2004/05, for example, the total interest costs on the national budget was $96.3 billion ($73.7 billion to local creditors) and $87.6 billion in 2005/06.[7] A similar scenario exists in commercial lending rate. Describing the lending spreads as "quite stubborn," deputy governor of the Bank of Jamaica, John Robinson, reported to Parliament's Public Administration and Appropriations Committee (PAAC) on Wednesday, October 29, 2014, that the "spreads now, and have for a very long time, remain very high . . .Average deposit rates are in the region of six per cent and average lending rates is 17 per cent." That average lending spread of 11 percent drew justified ire from PAAC committee member, Audley Shaw,[8] who to his credit, has led an assault on the high interest rate regime and through the JDX saved tax payers tens of billions of dollars as Finance Minister.

The follow-up questions to the current economic programme are, Will it be enough to guarantee that Jamaica will be pulled permanently back from the brink? Will its achievement lead to a better quality of life for all Jamaicans and sustainable development for the country? Will it reduce crime, corruption, tax dodging, high interest rates, and social and economic injustice? Will the borrowing subside? And after all the painful side effects that are being visited like a plague upon the people, what are the guarantees that the repetitive cycle of economic frustration will finally end? This latest round of borrowing arrangement with the International Monetary Fund is not Jamaica's first. Can our leaders ensure that it will be our last?

To find answers to these questions and lasting resolutions to these challenges, there must be conscientious efforts to bind the country's present and future leaders to macroeconomic prudence and social justice with the law and provide appropriate sanctions for breaches. Jamaica must finally correct its historical economic injustices. Therefore in addition to the economic fixes that are being vigorously pursued and the quest for growth in certain industries, the government must move with the same alacrity to institute the mechanisms for

---

[4] Alarming Statistics Re Jamaican Tax Reform, Money Max 101
[5] Ibid.
[6] Jamaica Information Service, Shaw Warns Against Tax Evasion, April 4, 2009
[7] Collister, Keith, Low Interest Rates the Key to 2005 Budget, Sunday Gleaner, April 3, 2005
[8] Luton, Daraine, Banks Make Interest Rates Killing, The Gleaner, Friday, October 31, 2014

1. *land reforms*, to reduce crime by moving definitively to end the problems of widespread landlessness, squatting and poor housing conditions;

2. *a just and equitable tax regime*, designed to improve revenue collection as well as to stem state-sanctioned economic injustice and balance the cost of financing public services and the social and economic infrastructural needs of the country;

3. *a single anti-corruption agency* with prosecutorial powers, to rein in corruption in public and private spheres in the Jamaican society;

4. *an autonomous local government system*, which will force Jamaicans to take greater responsibility for their own development and find their own solutions to personal and community needs;

5. *labour reforms*, for the "raising of the enthusiasm" and productivity of Jamaican business enterprises and workers;

6. *a more responsive governance system*, with the appropriate checks and balances to stem corruption and hold leaders accountable to the people for their stewardship between elections; and

7. *an effective court system*, which is accessible, timely, and fair.

These must all be grounded in a new constitutional framework that gives rise to the rapid enactment of the supporting legislative framework, the speedy activation of requisite state agencies, and the application of appropriate systems of accountability and sanctions. If these cannot be achieved, then it will not be long before the start of another epidemic of economic pain accompanied by another wicked wave of austerity measures and copious globules of bitter medicine. The vaccination that Jamaica needs is constitutional transformation. And again, it must be stated clearly that administrative tinkering is grossly irresponsible, if not patently deceitful.

REFORMATION OR REVOLUTION

Based on its population size, Jamaica is possibly the most recognizable country in the world. On the same basis, it is perhaps the most culturally influential. The island is geographically well positioned in the center of the Americas and strategically situated to function as an important hub for culture, travel, and trade. The well-travelled Christopher Columbus had described Jamaica as the most beautiful place he had ever seen. Half a millennium later, this was affirmed by Errol Flynn. The country remains a tourist magnet of sea, sand, and sunlight and it abounds in indigenous flora and fauna. The people are attractive, hospitable, lively, and ambitious. Jamaicans are also remarkably gifted for creativity, innovation, and intellectual and athletic dominance. The Jamaican brand is strong globally and the culture is infectious.

> Jamaicans enjoy better opportunities, better wages, and better legal protection in most other places than in their own land. The painful truth is that in Jamaica, "the poor do not have equality before the law; and, what is worse, they know it."

Notwithstanding the penchant for self-abasement, self-hate, political tribalism, and internal discord, given the scope for equal opportunities and fair wages, Jamaicans tend to thrive wherever they are planted in other countries across the globe. Jamaicans feature prominently in the political, social, and economic life of several countries in the diaspora. So why must Jamaica languish in social decay and persistent poverty? The answer is that Jamaicans enjoy better opportunities, better wages, and better legal protection in most other places than in their own land. In the words of Michael Manley, the painful truth is that in Jamaica, "the poor do not have equality before the law; and, what is worse, they know it."[9]

Law must respond to social and economic challenges. Sir Henry Sumner Maine was unequivocal in his declaration that "the movement of the progressive societies has hitherto been a movement from Status to Contract."[10] This simply means that genuine development requires that the society must move away from its class-defined social structures and achieve an equitable legal framework as the basis of its political, social, and economic engagements.

More than fifty years after independence, Jamaica has not successfully shaken off its colonial hierarchical social class organization to establish a more egalitarian legal framework. The equality that is paraded on paper eludes the vast majority of Jamaicans in reality because the constitution has not activated systems of accountability and enforcement and the ill-suited Westminster system of government has been an indubitable hindrance to progress. Jamaica has not changed sufficiently since Independence, and the conclusions here remain the same as they were in 1974 when then–Prime Minister Michael Manley declared that

> [w]hen one considers the magnitude of the economic and attitudinal restructuring which our conditions demand, it becomes clear that the politics of conservatism and tinkering are not only irrelevant to our situation but represent an intolerable default of responsibility. Man can adjust by tinkering but he cannot transform. Nothing less than transformation can provide answers to the dilemmas within which we are currently trapped.[11]

A large critical mass of the Jamaican population currently appears to be in a "wait-and-see" mode, but the society is teetering over the edge. The people will tolerate so much and no more. If significant managed change is not realized over the short term, then the inevitable change might become unmanaged and unmanageable. In recent decades, this type of change has been seen through the dismantling of the Iron Curtain and the demolition of the Berlin Wall. The dramatic fall of repressive regimes in North Africa and disturbances elsewhere in the Arabic world also represent spectacular and modern examples of what *real* people power can achieve.

DECISION TIME

In October 2010, in an article under the title, *Jamaica's Economic Growth to 2015 Projected to be 7th Slowest in the World*, Steven Jackson summarized Jamaica's growth prospects in the following manner:

> No cranes dot the capital city's business centre, its roads are filled with holes similar to the tattered clothes of beggars at the stoplights, and oftentimes youth recite an expression that reflects a lack of opportunity—nothin' nah gwan'. Jamaica, however, can expect more of the same as it is projected to trail some 143 nations in the world in growth statistics, which is a barometer of prosperity. With projections of about 1.3 per cent annually over the next

---

9.   Manley, Michael, Politics of Change: 58–59
10. Maine, Ancient Law: 170, 1861
11. Manley, Michael, Politics of Change: 22

five years, the island will grow three times slower than the world economy, according to charts within the World Economic Outlook (WEO) published this month by the IMF.[12]

Whereas the Latin America and Caribbean region was projected to outperform the global economy with an average growth rate of 4.5 percent between 2010 and 2015, Jamaica's most optimist growth forecast was a nominal 1.3 percent *three times slower than the global economy.*[13]

The picture became more dismal, as Jackson highlighted the following factors:

1. Haiti, which is the poorest country in the Americas, was likely to grow twice as fast as Jamaica over the period under review.
2. Jamaica attracted foreign direct investment at a rate four times slower than the rest of the Caribbean between 2001 and 2008.
3. Jamaica's accumulated external debt grew twice as fast as the average for the Caribbean and sixteen times faster than Latin America during the same period.
4. Jamaica's trade deficit expanded at three times the rate of the Caribbean region.
5. Jamaica's Human Development Index (HDI) fell from 92 in 2006 to 100 in 2009.
6. Jamaica was also listed as one of the ten most difficult countries in the world to pay taxes, sitting ingloriously at 174 out of 183 countries.[14]

In its November 14, 2014, Press Release No. 14/519, entitled "IMF Staff Concludes Review Mission to Jamaica," the IMF projected growth at 2 percent for 2015/16. It also said that inflation is likely to remain at about 8 percent and unemployment was expected to hold steady at 13.8 percent.

There is no doubt that a 0.7 percent movement from 1.3 percent growth per annum to 2 percent is progress. However, Jamaica still falls below the average projected regional growth rate of 2.8 percent. Stronger Caribbean economies are expected to grow even faster.[15] Two-percent growth is not even a drop in the permeable pan of the Jamaican economy, and it cannot pull back the debt burden. There is every likelihood that the government will have to continue to borrow into the foreseeable future and expand the over two-trillion-dollar-debt burden.

These figures will have to change dramatically, and Jamaica's leaders must make a definitive decision on the economic destiny of their nation, once and for all. They must take the critical steps to rescue the nation and recover the hope of independence. The Jamaican society and economy are in desperate and dire straits, and hundreds of thousands of persons are suffering immeasurably. Under the current circumstances, conditions are likely to become worse long before they get better. "Vision 2030" is now looking more like a "Vision 2050."

> "Without growth and development the economy is going to stagnate."
>
> —P. J. Patterson

Danny Roberts, head of the Hugh Lawson Shearer Trade Union Education Institute (HLSTUEI), understands the price of austerity and has courageously stated that Jamaica is not likely to achieve

---

12. Jackson, Steven, Jamaica's Economic Growth to 2015 Projected to be 7th Slowest in the World, Business Observer, October 13, 2010
13. Ibid.
14. Ibid.
15. IMF, World Economic Outlook (WEO) Update, January 2014

sustainable growth any time soon. It is his assessment that it is the current economic programme that has given rise to stagnant wages, declining aggregate demand, weak labour market regulations, and high unemployment.[16] No economy can register sustainable growth under such circumstances, and former Prime Minister P. J. Patterson has advised that "without growth and development the economy is going to stagnate."[17]

Nevertheless, there is hope. Over the last thirty years, the world has been witness to some unprecedented turnarounds in the fortunes of many countries. Democracy has dug deep roots in the formerly repressive regimes in Eastern Europe. Peace has planted a strong foothold in Central America, which was notorious for armed civil strife. Measurable growth is evident in previously pauperized portions of Africa, and blooms of prosperity are unfurling in traditionally poverty-stricken sections of South America. Genuine democracy, abiding peace, and measurable growth are indeed realizable; and some of those countries have pulled their societies back from even worse conditions. Jamaica can also prosper.

The BRICS countries represent noteworthy studies in social and economic advancement through constitutional reforms. Jamaica should take careful stock. In two decades, Brazil slashed its poverty rates by half, lifted 28 million people out of extreme poverty and created scope for 36 million of its citizens to enter the middle class.[18] Russia stripped off its sluggish, state-centric bear coat, donned a more democratic business suit, halted steady economic decline, and registered impressive and consistent economic growth. India rebounded from near default on its loans in 1990 to become one of the world's fastest-growing economies today. China slashed extreme poverty from 84 percent of the population in 1981 to 12 percent by 2010, moved 700 million people out of economic desperation, and rose from the global economic scrapheap to become the fastest-growing and second most influential economy in the world.[19] South Africa has shed the scourge of apartheid and has since been realizing considerable economic advancement.

K. P. Krishnan noted in *India's Constitution and the Economy* that the "single-most important reform in the financial markets, namely dematerialization of financial instruments . . . and [the] creation of a national market was made possible only after an amendment tothe Constitution."[20] In 1988, China modified its communist economic structure with one significant new paragraph in its constitution. Article 1, Article 11 provides that

> [t]he state permits the private sector of the economy to exist and develop within the limits prescribed by law. The private sector of the economy is a complement to the socialist public economy. The state protects the lawful rights and interests of the private sector of the economy, and exercises guidance, supervision and control over the private sector of the economy.

Change does not have to be chaotic. Significant progressive social change can in fact result from legal reform processes. In all the regions and countries listed above, progress has resulted largely

---

16. Sustainable Growth Not Achievable with IMF Agreement, says Danny Roberts, The Jamaica Observer, December 14, 2014
17. Myers, Garfield, 'I Am Well Aware of the IMF Constraints', The Jamaica Observer, December 17, 2014
18. de Sainte Croix, Sarah, Brazil Strives for Economic Equality, The Rio Times, February 7, 2012
19. Here's How Much Poverty Has Declined in China, China Real Time, The Wall Street Journal, April 18, 2013,
20. Krishnan, K. P., India's Constitution and the Economy

from managed change through constitutional reforms. The human longing after freedom from repression and oppression cannot be suppressed indefinitely; and where these changes have been resisted by the leaders in other countries, bloody, chaotic change—which has not advanced social or economic prospects—has ensued. The so-called Arab Spring is the most recent example.

Surely it is within the power of the leaders and people of Jamaica to pull the country peacefully back from the brink. One thing is certain: Jamaica cannot continue with the same levels of brazen exploitation of the masses, at the same growth rate or volumes of indebtedness that have been evident over the past two decades. Economic exploitation must be exposed and contained, class inequality must be eliminated, corruption must be curtailed, poverty must be eradicated, murders must end, the debt must be cut, and the general social and economic decline must be halted.

Under the existing macroeconomic design, regardless of how hard they work and how much effort or sacrifices they make, no significant progress will be realized by the broader mass of people for the foreseeable future. The taxes they pay will not be used to provide social services. It will continue to be funneled into the profits of the wealthy through debt payment and the grossly unjust economic system. Their community roads will continue to deteriorate, their schools and hospitals will continue to be under-resourced and the economy will continue to register low and negative growth. Jamaica cannot continue to do the same wrong things and expect different results. It has been twelve administrations and in excess of fifty years of the same depressive cycle. It is time for the yoke to be lifted. It is time for real change. It is full time for Jamaica to prosper.

NOW IS THE TIME

The irony in social and economic repression is that those who stand to lose the most through rebellion, riots, revolts, and revolution are the ones who are in the best position to gain even more from progressive reformation; yet they are the ones who resist the most. A more stable society gives rise to greater economic growth, and growth often benefits the entrepreneurs. In a revolution, there are many losers. In a reformation, everyone can win.

> The irony in social and economic repression is that those who stand to lose the most through rebellion, riots, revolts and revolution are the ones who are in the best position to gain even more from progressive reformation; yet they are the ones who resist the most.

The best legacy that Jamaica's current political leaders can create is a genuinely just, equitable, democratic, and economically prosperous society. "Now is time, this is the hour" for all the country's leaders to sit down, beyond narrow partisanship and political one-upmanship, to craft the constitutional framework and activate the systems of accountability that can lay the basis for genuine development for *all* Jamaicans. This can be done out of a sincere concern for the progress of the nation, out of a patriotic commitment to a brighter and better Jamaica, or pragmatically out of the pressing need to avert the looming social catastrophe.

Jamaica has run out of alternatives. There are essentially only two choices left: revolutionary change with chaos or transformational change without chaos. Tinkering and incrementalism are no longer viable options. Constitutional reform is certainly no panacea. It will not, of itself, resolve all the nation's problems, but the constitution is the foundation of society and it represents the ideal place to start on the pathway to a New Jamaica. Reforms must also be accompanied by progressive, patriotic leadership that is committed to social and economic justice. However, resolution cannot begin without a sound constitutional template. If Jamaica's leaders cannot get it right on paper, there is little chance they will ever get it right in practice.

> Given the right combination of leadership and reforms, Jamaica could rebound economically and begin to enjoy prosperity within a decade.

It is unfortunate that Jamaica should have fallen into such a wretched economic shape because many of the politicians understand the economic class dynamics and know well what the country's problems are and where the solutions lie. It is time that they come together across the political divides to fix them. Based on the pace of the progress made in the BRICS nations, and with a significantly smaller population than all the growing economies referenced in this research, given the right combination of patriotic leadership and reforms, Jamaica could rebound economically and begin to enjoy prosperity within a decade. Recovery could even be quicker with the buy-in of the general population and the cooperation of the moneyed classes.

Father of the nation and national hero Norman Manley made it clear that

> [t]here is a common mass in this country whose interest must predominate above and beyond all other classes. No man is democratic, no man is a sincere and honest democrat who does not accept the elementary principle that the object of civilization is to raise the standard of living and security of the masses of the people. If you do not agree with that principle, then you are playing with the words when you talk about democratic politics.[21]

It is not right for leaders to cause their people to suffer needlessly, and for so long. Heroes and celebrated leaders are those who take up the causes of the oppressed, and no society can advance without sacrificial and enlightened leadership. All Jamaica's leaders, in the public and private sector—in academia, trade unions, the professional associations, civic groups, the media, and the church—must stop playing with phrases, pandering to the privileged, and prevaricating the pain of the people. It is within their power to band together to demand the transformation that will overhaul the governance structure, halt the rampant exploitation of the broader mass of the people, and grow the economy. They must step up to the plate and claim justice for their people.

Many persons are only too willing to point fingers, find fault, and lay blame at the feet of the politicians. However, Jamaica could not have arrived at its present predicament if all its leaders had been playing their roles effectively. Political leaders cannot keep a democratic country where it does not collectively desire to be. The days of the messianic, all-powerful boss-leader have passed and the present prime minister cannot mother the entire nation to health by herself. She has recognized this and issued an impassioned invitation, at her inauguration in January 2012, for "all hands on deck." Real change has always resulted from genuine, progressive, broad-based people movements, and every patriotic Jamaican everywhere with a voice must speak up and speak out and join the fight for economic justice and the reconstruction of their nation.

Jamaicans can collectively choose to lumber along as we have for the last forty years at average growth of less than 1 percent, or even worse at the net negative growth for the last seven years. The

---

21.   Speech at the Launch of the PNP at Ward Theatre, September 18, 1938

people can choose to accept and applaud 2 percent growth as some kind of monumental achievement and then cross their fingers and pray that there will be no internal disruption, natural disasters, or external economic shocks. Or they can come together now, hold their leaders to account to correct the economic inequalities that will result in the transformation that could quite conceivably propel the economy to register 6 or 8 percent growth per annum, and usher in a prosperous future.

> Jamaica could not have arrived at its present predicament if all its leaders had been playing their roles effectively. Political leaders cannot keep a democratic country where it does not collectively desire to be.

Invariably, there will be those among the economic elites and within the elected and appointed aristocracy who will try to frustrate transformation efforts because of their fear of loss of power and prestige, but John F. Kennedy has warned that "those who make peaceful revolution impossible will make violent revolution inevitable."[22] In the end, however, the only sustainable development is equitable development, and Prime Minister Simpson Miller is absolutely correct—growth is not possible without poverty reduction. Jamaica will never realize its economic potential until it restructures its economic and governance dynamics. Recovery is not likely to materialize without reformation.

Jamaica *can* recover and prosper. There *is* still time; but not much. *"Now is the time, this is the hour . . ."*

Do the nation's leaders possess the good sense, initiative, and backbone for managed transformational change? Will they continue to tinker and procrastinate until the inevitable change overtakes them and they are swept aside in the tide? Or will they choose change without chaos?

[22.] Remarks on the first anniversary of the Alliance for Progress, March 13, 1962, at the White House

REFERENCES

Evan, William M. 1965. *"Law as an Instrument of Social Change."* p. 354 in Vago, Steven. 2009. *Law & Society.*

Ginsberg, Morris. 1965. *On Justice in Society.* Ithaca, NY: Cornell University Press

Greenberg, Jack. 1959. *Race Relations and American Law.* New York: Columbia University Press

Holmes, Oliver Wendell. 1897. "The Path of the Law," *Harvard Law Review,* 10 (March): 1963

Lewis, Allen (Sir). *The Separation of Powers—Its Relevance Parliamentary Democracy* (1978) WILJ 4

Maine, 1861 *Ancient Law,* Lillian Goldman Law Library http://avalon.law.yale.edu/subject_menus/maineaco.asp

Manley, Michael. 1974. *Politics of Change,* Kent: Andre Deutsch

Milo Vandemoortele and Kate Bird 2010. *Progress in Economic Conditions in Mauritius: Success against the odds.* London: Overseas Development Institute

Nettleford, Rex. 1971. *Manley and the New Jamaica,* London: Longman Caribbean

Pound, Roscoe. 1914. "Justice According to the Law", *Columbia Law Review,* 14 (1): 1–26. 1941

Sumner, William G. 1906. *Folkways,* Boston: Ginn and Co.

Vago, Steven. 2009. *Law & Society.* New Jersey: Pearson Education, Inc.

Ward, Lester. 1906. *Applied Sociology,* Boston: Ginn and Co.

REPORTS CITED

CIA World FactBook 2014, *http://www.theodora.com/wfbcurrent/jamaica/jamaica_international_rankings_2014.html*

Final Report of the Joint Select Committee of the Houses of Parliament on Constitutional and Electoral Reform

IMF, World Economic Outlook (WEO) Update, January 2014

Jamaica Crime and Safety Report, 2012, US State Department Report

Jamaica Economic Performance Assessment, USAID Report, May 2008

Jamaica Poverty and Wealth, Information about Poverty and Wealth in Jamaica, *http://www.nationsencyclopedia.com/economies/Americas/Jamaica-POVERTY-AND-WEALTH.html#ixzz1wep5yE80*

Justice System Reform Task Force, Final Report, 2007

Ministry of Local Government and Community Development, Local Government Reform

PIOJ Report, November, 2011

Report of the Commission of Enquiry, into the Extradition Request for Christopher Coke, p. 56

Statistical Institute of Jamaica, *http://statinja.gov.jm/default.aspx*

US News and World Report, *http://thesocietypages.org/socimages/*

CASES CITED

IJCHR v Syringa Marshall-Burnett, Privy Council Appeal No. 41 of 2004

Pratt and Morgan v. Attorney General for Jamaica, [1993] 1 UKPC 1

CONSTITUTIONS REVIEWED

The Canada Act 1982

The Constitution Act of New Zealand, 1986

The Constitution of the Federative Republic of Brazil 1988

The Constitution of Jamaica 1962

The Constitution of the People's Republic of China 1982

The Constitution of the Republic of Cuba 1992

The Constitution of the Republic of South Africa 1996

The Constitution of the Sovereign Socialist Secular Democratic Republic of India, 2011

LEGISLATION CITED

The Employment (Equal Pay for Men and Women) Act 1975 of Jamaica

The Employment Equity Act 1998 of the Republic of South Africa

The Employment Equity Act of Canadian

The Law on the Protection of the Right and Interests of Women of the People's Republic of China

The Minimum Wage Act 1974 of Jamaica

ONLINE RESOURCES CITED

Again, Austerity Will Not Bring Economic Growth! Editorial, The Jamaica Observer, November 9, 2014, *http://www.jamaicaobserver.com/editorial/Again--austerity-will-not-bring-economic-growth-_17899187*

Alarming Statistics Re Jamaican Tax Reform, Money Max 101, *http://moneymax101.com/20120318/alarming-statistics-re-jamaican-tax-reform/*

Bailey, Tamara, Jamaica's Poverty Rating Worsens, The Gleaner, March 26, 2014, http://jamaica-gleaner.com/gleaner/20140326/news/news2.html

Best, Tony, *Joint CCJ in Trinidad and Tobago,* The New York Carib News, May 3, 2012, *http://www.nycaribnews.com/news.php?viewStory=1895*

Boyne, Ian, *The Creditors' Budget,* Sunday Gleaner, May 13, 2012

Claude Clarke, *What Will Fuel our Growth?* In Focus, The Sunday Gleaner, August 24, 2014, *http://jamaica-gleaner.com/gleaner/20140824/focus/focus2.html*

Clayton, Anthony, *A New Approach: National Security Policy for Jamaica,* quoted by James, Ewin, in The Economic Cost of Crime, The Jamaica Observer, Saturday, March 02, 2013

Countryeconomy.com, *Jamaica National Debt,* http://countryeconomy.com/national-debt/jamaica

Cummings, Victor, *The Problem of Squatting in Jamaica,* The Gleaner, May 24, 2009, *http://mobile.jamaicagleaner.com/20090524/news/news1.php*

de Sainte Croix, *Sarah, Brazil Strives for Economic Equality,* The Rio Times, February 7, 2012, *http://riotimesonline.com/brazil-news/rio-business/brazil-strives-for-economic-equality/#*

DiSchino, Christopher, *Affirmative Action in Brazil: Reverse Discrimination and the Creation of Constitutionally Protected Color-line,* University of Miami, International and Comparative Law Review, 2010, *https://litigation-essentials.lexisnexis.com/webcd/app?action=DocumentDisplay&craw lid=1&doctype=cite&docid=17+U.+Miami+Int'l+%26+Comp.+L.+Rev.+155&srctype=smi&srcid=3 B15&key=ae3d4cc0e7d9645c53050a04c6122aa3*

Douglas, Eisenhower, *Sovereignity, Independence and the Caribbean Court of Justice,* Dominica News Online, *http://dominicanewsonline.com/news/homepage/features/commentary/sovereignity-independence-caribbean-court-justice/*

Economic Oversight Committee worried about Gov't's under spending, Gleaner, December 9, 2014

Eichelberger, Erika, *The Head of the IMF Says Inequality Threatens Democracy,* Mother Jones, May 28, 2014, *http://www.motherjones.com/mojo/2014/05/imf-christine-lagarde-income-inequality*

Here's How Much Poverty Has Declined in China, China Real Time, The Wall Street Journal, April 18, 2013, *http://blogs.wsj.com/chinarealtime/2013/04/18/heres-how-much-poverty-has-declined-in-china/*

Higgins, Garfield, Ja's Political Immune System Has Been Terribly Compromised, The Jamaica Observer, December 14, 2014, *http://www.jamaicaobserver.com/columns/Ja-s-political-immune-system-has-been-terribly-compromised_18089194*

In spite of Criticism, Portia says Still Committed to Poor, The Gleaner, July 24, 2013, *http://jamaica-gleaner.com/gleaner/20130724/news/news81.html*

Jackson, Steven, *Jamaica's Economic Growth to 2015 Projected to be 7th Slowest in the World,* Business Observer, October 13, 2010, *http://www.jamaicaobserver.com/business/Jamaica-s-economic-growth-to-2015-projected-to-be-7th-slowest-in-the-world_8046873*

Jackson, Steven, *Study Finds Uneven Tax Rates Among Rich and Poor in Jamaica,* The Business Observer, November 9, 2014, *http://www.jamaicaobserver.com/business/Study-finds-uneven-tax-rates-among-rich-and-poor-in-Jamaica_17891770*

Jamaica falls on Corruption Perception Index, The Gleaner, December 4, 2014, *http://jamaica-gleaner.com/gleaner/20141204/lead/lead5.html*

J'cans Want Direct Vote for PM, The Gleaner, October 17, 2014, *http://jamaica-gleaner.com/gleaner/20141017/lead/lead2.html*

Kong, Basil Waine, *Creating Value of Dead Real estate in Jamaica,* February 16, 2010, *http://jamaicachapter.blogspot.com/2010/02/creating-value-out-of-dead-real-estate.html*

Krishnan, K. P., *India's Constitution and the Economy*, http://www.india-seminar. com/2013/642/642_k_p_krishnan.htm

Luton, Daraine, *Banks Make Interest Rates Killing*, The Gleaner, Friday, October 31, 2014, http:// jamaica-gleaner.com/gleaner/20141031/news/news2.html

Meikle, Ashford W., *Is the CCJ a Trojan Horse?* The Gleaner, December 26, 2010, http://jamaica-gleaner.com/gleaner/20101226/cleisure/cleisure2.html

Sustainable Growth Not Achievable with IMF Agreement, says Danny Roberts, The Jamaica Observer, December 14, 2014, http://www.jamaicaobserver.com/MOBILE/NEWS/ Sustainable-growth-not-achievable-with-IMF-Agreement--says-Danny-Roberts

Myers, Garfield, *'I Am Well Aware of the IMF Constraints'*, The Jamaica Observer, December 17, 2014, http://www.jamaicaobserver.com/news/-I-am-well-aware-of-the-IMF-constraints-_18109562

Myers, Garfield, *PNP Mayor Calls for Multi-party Democracy*, The Jamaica Observer, December 11, 2014, http://www.jamaicaobserver.com/news/Damaging-tribalism_18088401

Navarro, Luis Hernandez, *Bolivia has transformed itself by ignoring the Washington Consensus*, p://www.guardian.co.uk/commentisfree/cifamerica/2012/mar/21/bolivia-washington-consensus?INTCMP=SRCH http://www.indexmundi.com/g/g.aspx?v=74&c=jm&l=en

Parents, Teachers Most Trusted, Says Poll, The Jamaica Observer, September 22, 2010, http://www. jamaicaobserver.com/news/Parents--teachers-most-trusted--says-poll_7982328

Powell, Lawrence A., Lewis, Balford A. and Seligson, Mitchell A., *Political Culture of Democracy in Jamaica, 2010, Democratic Consolidation in the Americas in Hard Times*, quoted by Gareth Manning in *Jamaica scores Big on Corruption*, The Sunday Gleaner, April 26, 2009, http:// jamaica-gleaner.com/gleaner/20090426/news/news6.html

Poverty, income inequality on the rise in Jamaica – Report, The Business Gleaner, October 9, 2011, http://jamaica-gleaner.com/gleaner/20111009/business/business8.html

Robotham, Don, *Jamaica on the Brink*, In Focus, The Sunday Gleaner, October 21, 2012, http:// jamaica-gleaner.com/gleaner/20121021/focus/focus1.html

Robinson, Gordon, *My Vote of No Confidence*, In Focus, The Sunday Gleaner, November 23, 2014, http://jamaica-gleaner.com/gleaner/20141123/focus/focus1.html

Shaw Warns against Tax Evasion, Jamaica Information Service, April 4, 2009, http://jis.gov.jm/ shaw-warns-against-tax-evasion/

Sustainable Growth Not Achievable with IMF Agreement, says Danny Roberts, The Jamaica Observer, December 14, 2014, http://www.jamaicaobserver.com/news/ Sustainable-growth-not-achievable-with-IMF-Agreement--says-Danny-Roberts

Trading Economics, *Net Migration in Jamaica*, http://www.tradingeconomics.com/jamaica/net-migration-wb-data.html

APPENDIX 1

Extended Summary of Jamaica's Worrying Development Indices

Jamaica's Worrying Development Indices
1. Jamaica's average national growth has been about 0.8 percent over the last 40 years.
2. Jamaica was ranked at number 176 out of 179 on the list of debt to GDP in 2013 *(Countryeconomy.com)*. In 2014 the debt climbed to over $2 trillion.
3. Jamaica's debt payment was approximately 43 percent of the Budget for 2014-15. Every Jamaican now owes over $700,000.
4. Jamaica had the highest bond interest in the world in May 2012 *(Center for Economic and Policy Research)*.
5. Jamaica's exchange rate stood at over JA $114 to US $1 at the end of 2014
6. Jamaica's GDP per capita is about 40 percent of Barbados'. In 2011, it was US $8,300 per annum. Barbados' was at US $21,800 *(United Nation's Human Development Report)*.
7. Jamaica had the second worst income disparity in the Region for 2011, and among the worst in the world. Jamaica's Gini coefficient (income disparity measurement) is 59.9, behind Haiti at 59.2, and only topped by Suriname at 61.6 *(IMF Report)*.
8. Jamaica's rich is actually getting richer while the poor is really getting poorer. Jamaica's Gini coefficient was 45.5 in 2004 *(CIA World Factbook)*. It was 59.9 in 2011 *(IMF)*. There has actually been a significant transfer of wealth in recent years.
9. Jamaica was perceived as the most corrupt country in the western hemisphere in 2009 *(The Political Culture of Democracy in Jamaica)*. Jamaica was ranked at 3.3 on the Corruption Perception Index, CPI, in 2011 *(Transparency International)*.
10. Jamaica has nearly one-fifth of its population or 540,000 persons living in squatter settlements *(Ministry of Housing)*.
11. Jamaica is the second most poverty-stricken nation in the region: 17.6 percent of Jamaicans were living in poverty in 2010 *(PIOJ)*, 43% of Jamaicans survived on about J $200 per day in 2010 *(IMF)*, 14.4 percent of Jamaicans survived on less than $2 US dollars a day in 2011 *(World Bank)*.
12. Jamaica had the second-highest unemployment rate in the region in 2010; 13.8 percent of Jamaicans were unemployed in 2014 *(Statin)*.

THE NEW ZEALAND CITIZENS' CHARTER
SECTION FOUR: CITIZENS' CHARTER
Preamble:

The nation is a cooperative body; all citizens have certain inalienable rights, but all adult citizens also have certain duties to the State. Therefore, every law court, tribunal or body of adjudication shall use the Citizens' Charter as a basis for comparison between the rights of each person as guaranteed under this Constitution, and the duties of each person to the State, as summarised below.

All citizens have a duty:

1) To take responsibility for their actions, wherever reasonable.
2) To endeavour to provide the best support for their children, families, associates and culture.
3) To help meet the costs of running the nation, and to minimise their reliance on State assistance.
4) To be ethical and compassionate in their daily activities, and foster those values in their families.
5) To make good use of learning institutions and encourage their children to do the same.
6) To provide a safe and loving home environment for themselves and others wherever possible.
7) To respect the rights of others.
8) To understand that the Government can only ever be a reflection of the people who create it, and therefore to take every reasonable step to support wholesome Government activities, while always vigorously opposing arbitrary, callous, cruel or bureaucratic rule.
9) To understand the politics of the day, and to vote according to their consciences
10) To live with a sensitive understanding of the ecosphere in which we live, and understand how we, as individuals and as a group, affect the world around us.
11) To help provide help for those in need.
12) To oppose conflict both locally and internationally, but be prepared to take a firm moral stand against injustice.
13) To reach their full potential as human beings.
14) Limitation:
    Nothing in this section shall permit the imposition of arbitrary or otherwise unreasonable standards of behaviour upon any person or group.

THE LABOUR LAWS IN THE CONSTITUTION OF THE FEDERATIVE REPUBLIC OF BRAZIL

CHAPTER II - SOCIAL RIGHTS

Article 6. Education, health, work, leisure, security, social security, protection of motherhood and childhood, and assistance to the destitute, are social rights, as set forth by this Constitution.

Article 7. The following are rights of urban and rural workers, among others that aim to improve their social conditions:

I. employment protected against arbitrary dismissal or against dismissal without just cause, in accordance with a supplementary law which shall establish severance-pay, among other rights;

II. unemployment insurance, in the event of involuntary unemployment;

III. severance-pay fund;

IV. nationally unified minimum wage, established by law, capable of satisfying their basic living needs and those of their families with housing, food, education, health, leisure, clothing, hygiene, transportation and social security, with periodical adjustments to maintain its purchasing power, it being forbidden to use it as an index for any purpose;

V. a salary floor in proportion to the extent and complexity of the work;

VI. irreducibility of the wages, except when established in collective agreement or covenant;

VII. guarantee of wages never below the minimum one, for those receiving variable pay;

VIII. year-end one-salary bonus based on the full pay or on the amount of the pension;

IX. payrate for night-shift work higher than that for daytime work;

X. wage protection, as provided by law, with felonious withholding c. wages being a crime;

XI. participation in the profits or results, independent of wages, and, exceptionally, participation in the management of the company, defined by law;

XII. family allowance for their dependents;

XIII. normal working hours not exceeding eight hours per day a forty-four hours per week, with the option of compensating working hours a reducing the length of the workday through an agreement or a collection bargaining covenant;

XIV. a workday of six hours for work carried out in continuous s} unless otherwise established by collective bargaining;

XV. paid weekly leave, preferably on Sundays;

XVI. rate of pay for overtime at least fifty per cent higher than that of normal work;

XVII. annual vacation with remuneration at least one third higher than the normal salary;

XVIII.   maternity leave without loss of job and of salary, for a period of one hundred and twenty days;

XIX.   paternity leave, under the terms established by law;

XX.   protection of the labour market for women through specific incentives, as provided by law;

XXI.   advance notice of dismissal in proportion to the length of service of at least thirty days, as provided by law;

XXII.   reduction of employment related risks by means of health, hygiene and safety rules;

XXIII.   additional remuneration for strenuous, unhealthy or dangerous work, as established by law;

XXIV.   retirement pension;

XXV.   free assistance for children and dependents from birth to six years of age, in day-care centres and pre-school facilities;

XXVI.   recognition of collective bargaining agreements and covenants;

XXVII.   protection on account of automation, as established by law;

XXVIII.   occupational accident insurance, to be paid for by the employer, without excluding the employer's liability for indemnity in the event of malice or fault;

XXIX.   legal action with respect to credits arising from employment relationships with a limitation of:

        a.   five years for urban workers, up to the limit of two years after the end of the employment contract;

        b.   up to two years after the end of the contract for rural workers;

XXX.   prohibition of any difference in wages, in the performance of duties and in hiring criteria by reason of sex, age, colour or marital status;

XXXI.   prohibition of any discrimination with respect to wages and hiring criteria of handicapped workers;

XXXII.   prohibition of any distinction between manual, technical and intellectual work or among the respective professionals;

XXXIII.   prohibition of night, dangerous or unhealthy work for minors under eighteen years of age, and of any work for minors under fourteen years of age, except as an apprentice;

XXXIV.   equal rights for workers with a permanent employment bond and for sporadic workers.

Sole paragraph - The category of domestic servants is ensured of the rights set forth in items IV, VI, VIII, XV, XVII, XVIII, XIX, XXI and XXIV, as well as of integration in the social security system.

Article 8. Professional or union association is free, with regard for the following:

I.   the law may not require authorization of the State for a union to be founded, except for authorization for registration with the competent agency. it being forbidden to the Government the interference and the intervention in the union;

II.   it is forbidden to create more than one union, at any level representing a professional or economic category, in the same territorial base, which shall be defined by the workers or employers concerned, which base may not cover less than the area of one municipality;

III.   it falls to the union to defend the collective or individual rights and interests of the category, including legal or administrative disputes;

IV.   the general assembly shall establish the contribution which, in the case of a professional category, shall be discounted from the payroll, to support the confederative system of the respective union representation, regardless of the contribution set forth by law;

V.   no one shall be required to join or to remain a member of a union;

VI.   the collective labor bargainings must be held with the participation of unions;

VII.   retired members shall be entitled to vote and be voted on in unions;

VIII.   the dismissal of a unionised employee is forbidden from the moment of the registration of his candidacy to a position of union direction or representation and, if elected, even if as a substitute, up to one year after the end of his term in office, unless he commits a serious fault as established by law

Sole paragraph - The provisions of this article apply to the organization of rural unions and those of fishing communities, with due regard for the conditions established by law.

Article 9. The right to strike is guaranteed, it being the competence of workers to decide on the advisability of exercising it and on the interests to defended thereby.

Paragraph 1. The law shall define the essential services or activities shall provide with respect to the satisfaction of the community's undelayable needs.

Paragraph 2. The abuses committed shall subject those responsible to penalties of the law.

Article 10. The participation of workers and employers is ensured in collegiate bodies of government agencies in which their professional or so security interests are subject of discussion and resolution.

Article 11. It is ensured, in companies with more than 200 employees, I election of a representative of the employees for the exclusive purpose furthering direct negotiations with the employers.

ECONOMIC DEVELOPMENT IN THE CONSTITUTION OF THE PEOPLE'S REPUBLIC OF CHINA

Article 14. The state continuously raises labour productivity, improves economic results and develops the productive forces by enhancing the enthusiasm of the working people, raising the level of their technical skill, disseminating advanced science and technology, improving the systems of economic administration and enterprise operation and management, instituting the socialist system of responsibility in various forms and improving organization of work. The state practises strict economy and combats waste. The state properly apportions accumulation and consumption, pays attention to the interests of the collective and the individual as well as of the state and, on the basis of expanded production, gradually improves the material and cultural life of the people.

Article 15. The state practises economic planning on the basis of socialist public ownership. It ensures the proportionate and co-ordinated growth of the national economy through overall balancing by economic planning and the supplementary role of regulation by the market. Disturbance of the orderly functioning of the social economy or disruption of the state economic plan by any organization or individual is prohibited.

Article 16. State enterprises have decision-making power in operation and management within the limits prescribed by law, on condition that they submit to unified leadership by the state and fulfil all their obligations under the state plan. State enterprises practise democratic management through congresses of workers and staff and in other ways in accordance with the law.

Article 17. Collective economic organizations have decision-making power in conducting independent economic activities, on condition that they accept the guidance of the state plan and abide by the relevant laws. Collective economic organizations practise democratic management in accordance with the law, with the entire body of their workers electing or removing their managerial personnel and deciding on major issues concerning operation and management.

Article 18. The People's Republic of China permits foreign enterprises, other foreign economic organizations and individual foreigners to invest in China and to enter into various forms of economic co-operation with Chinese enterprises and other economic organizations in accordance with the law of the People's Republic of China. All foreign enterprises and other foreign economic organizations in China, as well as joint ventures with Chinese and foreign investment located in China, shall abide by the law of the People's Republic of China. Their lawful rights and interests are protected by the law of the People's Republic of China.

Edwards Brothers Malloy
Oxnard, CA USA
April 8, 2015